NO LONGER HOMELESS

NO LONGER HOMELESS

*How the Ex-Homeless Get and
Stay Off the Streets*

David Wagner

With Gemma Atticks

ROWMAN & LITTLEFIELD
Lanham • Boulder • New York • London

Published by Rowman & Littlefield
An imprint of
The Rowman & Littlefield Publishing Group, Inc.
4501 Forbes Boulevard, Suite 200, Lanham, Maryland 20706
https://rowman.com

Unit A, Whitacre Mews, 26-34 Stannary Street, London SE11 4AB,
United Kingdom

British Library Cataloguing in Publication Information Available

Library of Congress Cataloging-in-Publication Data

Names: Wagner, David, author. | Atticks, Gemma, 1981– author.
Title: No longer homeless : how the ex-homeless get and stay off the streets /
    David Wagner with Gemma Atticks.
Description: Lanham : Rowman & Littlefield, [2018] | Includes bibliographical
    references and index. |
Identifiers: LCCN 2017050528 (print) | LCCN 2017052783 (ebook) | ISBN
    9781538110089 (electronic) | ISBN 9781538110072 (cloth : alk. paper)
Subjects: LCSH: Homeless persons—United States. | Homeless persons—
    Employment—United States. | United States—Social policy.
Classification: LCC HV4505 (ebook) | LCC HV4505 .W234 2018 (print) |
    DDC 362.5/920973—dc23
LC record available at https://lccn.loc.gov/2017050528

Printed in the United States of America

CONTENTS

ACKNOWLEDGMENTS

As with other books that place us in a different world, in this case the world of the streets and those *who lived there and later exited them*, I was dependent on assistance in navigating my way around the areas studied. Several people and groups were most helpful: the Los Angeles Community Action Network in Skid Row LA; the Los Angeles Poverty Department (LAPD), a theater group and educational group; the Amistad Center in Portland, Maine, a multiservice program for people with mental disabilities; and the National Coalition for the Homeless (NCH) in Washington, DC. I particularly want to honor Michael Stoops of the NCH, whose untimely death occurred a short time after he had organized my interviews with the Speakers Bureau members. I also wish to thank the Emmaus Center in Haverhill, Massachusetts; the Crossroads Shelter in Portsmouth, New Hampshire; and the Homeless Voices for Justice at Preble Street Resource Center in Portland, Maine.

This book provided me with a good opportunity to work with Ms. Gemma Atticks, a superb student from the University of Southern Maine, who was not only gifted, but eager and hungry for knowledge and experience. As usual, I am indebted to Marcia B. Cohen, my wife, and expert on homelessness, who recently retired from the University of New England. She remains my first reader and audience.

I

GIVING VOICE TO THE EX-HOMELESS

Early in the 1980s "homelessness" was rediscovered in America. For a short period of that decade, the specter of Americans living on the streets, in cars and other vehicles, in abandoned housing, and elsewhere shocked Americans and caused controversy between activists and advocates on the one side, and the conservative Reagan administration on the other. Unfortunately, several decades later, while the problem has if anything grown worse and larger, the presence of homeless people is no longer shocking or upsetting to most Americans.

Although there are many reasons for the decline in attention to homelessness, one nagging issue is whether the problem was ever described adequately or defined in a way that could sustain interest. For both advocates and critics, the visible denizens of the streets and shelters became a focus, but over time as many people left the streets and became housed, while, of course, others died or ended up in institutions, the long-term fate of all those who were and would be homeless, at the lowest rung of poverty, was not explored.

The firm misconception was planted that the homeless people you happen to see on the street today were probably there last year, and would likely be there next year. In reality, although there are some people who are homeless for many years, they make up only a small part of the population,[1] and even those people labeled as "chronic homeless" often do get housing. Each year millions of people move from sleeping in cars or on the streets or doubled-up with relatives or friends to securing their own apartments or other housing. Social service agencies place many thousands of people in housing each day. Lost in the heated debates about the politics of homelessness is that for most people surviving on the streets is a temporary, albeit awful, phenomenon.

Some experts have tried to estimate the number of Americans who have experienced homelessness by surveys among the general population. They have reached estimates that, depending on exact definitions of homelessness, range in the area of between 6 percent and 14 percent of the whole US population, usually over a particular period such as five years.[2] This is an immense part of the population, ranging from nearly fourteen to as many as nearly thirty-two million people, using US Census figures and excluding children under fifteen. The issue of homelessness is one that is extremely broad, but it is not represented well by the "drunks" or "bag ladies" that many people associate with homelessness.

The time has come for a book on ex- or formerly homeless people. Of course, in the 1980s the dramatic issue seemed the idea of people living on the streets. But we now also know that despite all the awful conditions apparent on the streets (and in many shelters too) most homeless people return to housing and rejoin the domiciled poverty population. This book draws on those who have made it "out of homelessness" both to explore how they did so, but as importantly how they are living now, and what allows them to survive, if uneasily, in housing.

Looking at people who have been homeless not only provides us with valuable information about surviving the streets, but shows us the resilience and strength many poor people have. I suggest that it adds to our perception of the humanity of poor people by exploring their lives over time, in some cases, through many years of housing. Second, unlike the interviews of people while they are at a shelter or on the streets and at their most vulnerable, it also allows for reflection by people who have weathered and overcome difficult circumstances.

The book begins by reviewing some key issues about homelessness and sharing information about how we study the formerly homeless. My research methods are discussed more fully in appendix I. Chapter 2 shares interviews with formerly homeless people and illustrates how many of them surpass common expectations about the trajectory of a homeless person's life. In chapters 3–6, I address some of what the interviews make evident is needed for homeless people to remain off the streets: housing, income, and supportive communities. In appendix

II, I discuss many important people in American history who were formerly homeless, and a number of celebrities who say they were homeless.

In order to discuss people who are formerly homeless, it is necessary to give the reader some background on what homelessness looks like, what its causes are, and what some of the political conflicts around addressing it have been about.

WHO ARE THE HOMELESS?

Living in a large Western city, twenty-four-year-old Carolyn Burns (names have been changed to protect privacy) and her two young children barely got by month to month on a small welfare check and their food stamp allotment. Although she lived in public housing that once might have been considered one of the few "stable" forms of housing for poor people, Ms. Burns was served a notice that she would be evicted if she could not pay the new market rates proposed for her apartment by the federal government and a housing developer.[3] After some months of tenant protests and futile efforts to find housing nearby so her children could remain in their school, she was served with an eviction notice. Ms. Burns and her two children, Vera, seven, and Miles, five, trekked with their belongings to a city welfare office, where they were told they had no choice but to enter a homeless shelter downtown.

Mark, a forty-year-old divorced man, lived in a Midwestern industrial city once known for its factories and blue-collar workforce. Mark's job was cut years ago, leaving him and his wife Cathy in great debt due to her serious medical condition. Unable to afford their rent and her medication with no income, the two moved back to Mark's parents' house one hundred miles away. This experience was increasingly unpleasant for Mark; his parents blamed him for being out of work and for failing to pay the bills he and his wife had accumulated. Mark's drinking became worse and he stayed out of the house increasingly, hanging out with "the guys." One day after he arrived home at 3:00 a.m., his wife started yelling at him, and Mark left after the argument. At first he traveled throughout the region looking for work, occasionally picking up day labor and construction work. He would stay in cheap boarding houses and sometimes manage a place to stay with people he met. Blaming himself for his problems, he became increasingly depressed and even suicidal. He stopped looking for jobs and joined an encampment of mostly men near the railroad tracks. He never thought he would be a "hobo" and live with the wretched of the earth. But the acceptance he found there among people in a similar situation soothed his depression for a while.

Paula and Gabe were teenage sweethearts who had gone together since they were thirteen. Both teens did well in school until junior year. That year their goth hairdos and attire, as well as decreasing attention to their school work, marked them for ridicule from other students and increased frustration from their middle-class parents. A teacher tried to help Paula, urging her to continue to work hard despite being bullied and feeling like a "loser." But Gabe's life continued to feel as if it were unwinding; he could not stand going home or to school. One day after three "jocks" beat him up in school, Gabe decided he could not take living in the small Southern town anymore. Although Paula was reluctant, she agreed to go with him, and hitch rides up North with their backpacks and a small amount of money in their pockets. Life on the road was sure different; it was fun a lot of time as they met cool kids who did whatever they wanted and were hanging out in each large town they entered. It was like having friends all over. Occasionally, when they were separated from friends, it was a little scary as their money was going fast, and they were arrested twice for vagrancy. But generally the freedom of life and affiliation with the other kids who were "into" the same music, looks, and resistant attitude overcame some of the dreariness in their lives. They would travel for two years with only a minimal use of anything but their wits, their friends, shared money, and panhandling.

Carolyn (Burns), Mark, Paula, and Gabe have many differences. They differ by age, gender, and by ethnicity (Carolyn is African American, Mark Polish-Irish, and Paula and Gabe are white Anglo-Saxons), by the social class they came from (poor, working class, middle class), and by region in the United States (West, Midwest, South). Nevertheless, at least in the last few decades, they would share a status and a label as "homeless" people.[4]

Most Americans feel like they can identify who are the homeless and what their issues are. For many people, the stereotypical panhandler in shabby old clothes, with a long, scraggly beard and a modestly scratched-out sign, "will work for food" or "homeless veteran—Please Help!" represents the homeless population.[5] But the fact is the most visible homeless are often the least representative of the broader number of people who become homeless. Few homeless people actually panhandle (there are, of course, people who are not homeless but do panhandle), and the stereotype of the older man, particularly a white man, is a vestige of earlier eras when America had large "skid rows" of poor people, many of whom were elderly men, drunk or with other disabilities.[6]

There are some Americans who do know that millions of women with children are homeless, that young men particularly of color are a large percentage of the homeless population, and those teens and other young people form groups both on the streets and in lofts and apartments where they crash together. But the image of "a bum" or "hobo" remains tied to the public image of the homeless as a cultural icon. Efforts to "destigmatize" homelessness, which were particularly taken up by advocates in the 1980s, have often failed. It is a circular process in which those who seek to help the homeless or poor people differ from the public: those who are poor or who work with them see men, women, and children of different ages, races, and backgrounds every day, but the public tends to avoid the poor areas of town and sees mostly panhandlers or those whose presence on the streets creates problems, and hence makes the evening news.

The homeless are not only diverse by demographic characteristics; the word "homeless" camouflages many, many differences. There are, of course, people without homes who use shelters and other emergency facilities in America's cities and towns. But for everyone like Carolyn Burns and her children who enters a shelter, there are many more people who *never* enter a shelter. Hating the soul-stripping bureaucracy of a large shelter that intrudes into their lives, many homeless people, like Mark, find their own spaces with others, anywhere from "tent cities" (these are usually areas of town that have been taken over illegally by homeless people, although often tolerated; see for example, the recent film *Tent City, U.S.A.*)[7] to abandoned vehicles[8] to apartment buildings or garages or even "hobo jungles" in the woods; see Wasserman and Clair on homeless people's disdain for the shelter system.[9] And still others like Paula and Gabe are able to "couch surf" at friends' homes for long periods. Others are "doubled-up" (usually against land-lord policies) in an apartment with others. This means they may be sleeping on the floors or on couches or mats in crowded apartments. And then there are the people whom even homelessness scholars dispute whether they should be counted as homeless: people in jail and prison, group homes, or rehabilitation centers who have no homes to return to. Should they be considered homeless or not? Advocates often clash with government over the definition of homelessness, with the latter tending to reject those doubled-up with relatives or friends, living in vehicles, and those in jail or other institutions as being homeless, leaving a gap of many millions in a count of homeless people.[10]

There is another important variable about homelessness: how long one is homeless. Carolyn and her children may have been referred to a housing voucher program that quickly helped them get a new apartment, being homeless for only two weeks. Mark, plagued by alcoholism, and perhaps influenced by his new surroundings among the longer-term homeless, continued to be homeless after four years. Paula and Gabe eventually returned home after two years. Paula made up with her family and started working on a GED (General Equivalency Diploma for high school), while Gabe ran away from his parents and returned to the streets until he was twenty-one, when he met a new girlfriend and moved in with her. How to regard these differences? Carolyn and her children might be seen as very short-term homeless, but if she and the kids later had another round of homelessness (as poor families and individuals often do) they would be considered "episodically homeless" (reflecting the fact that many homeless people go through an episode or several episodes of homelessness rather than a permanent condition).[11] Mark appears as a long-term homeless person, or in the George W. Bush and Obama administrations' terminology, a "chronic homeless" person. The Bush administration decided to focus on "chronic homelessness," which was defined as being homeless for two years or more.[12] Many advocates did not like this term.[13] Paula and Gabe provide other issues to ponder. While their status may allow us to consider them homeless or even long-term homeless, should the availability of resources at home or some "voluntariness" to their homelessness be taken into account? Generally, youth homelessness is treated differently in the literature in both academia and social service; their issues are different from those of adults who are homeless. Although advocates demur at any mention of "voluntary homelessness," I have met a good number of people, most of them young and many more male than female, who do intentionally take "to the road" just as in the 1930s many young men "rode the rails" to seek jobs, money, and adventure (see Pippert for some sense of homeless men on the road).[14]

THE CAUSES OF HOMELESSNESS

After a lapse of about three and a half decades between the end of the Great Depression in America and the resurgence of both the terms *homeless* and *homelessness* in the late 1970s and 1980s, we have learned a lot about this unhappy state. Though there are obviously disagreements among academics and professional experts, most who have written about the homeless believe several major social factors that began in the 1970s all established the conditions for a rebirth of homelessness:

1. The decline of industrial labor in the United States (known to experts as *deindustrialization*) caused the United States to lose tens of millions of jobs such as steelworker, paper worker, electrical worker, maritime worker, autoworker, etc.; the new jobs have for the most part been low-paid service employee jobs in restaurants, motels and hotels, fast food outlets, discount chains such as Wal-Mart, and so on. These jobs are generally nonunion and poorly paid, and have few if any fringe benefits such as health insurance, vacations, sick time, and pensions. While there are people who were able to get in on the "dot.com" and other high-technology growth, those jobs increasingly required higher degrees. For people with less than a high school degree (and increasingly even college) who used to simply queue up at a mill or factory, there are very few job opportunities.[15]

2. There has been a steep decline in affordable housing, particularly in urban areas, while middle-class and rich people moved into the cities (known popularly as *gentrification*). A look at the average rents in the 1970s compared with today frequently gives my students heartburn. Far beyond inflation, rentals in cities such as New York; Boston; Washington, DC; Chicago; Miami; Cleveland; Seattle; Portland, Oregon; San Francisco; Los Angeles; and San

Diego have gone up by many multiples of zeros. Not just big cities, but also smaller places have seen a steady increase in rents and housing prices and a concomitant rise in homelessness. In New England, not only Portland, Maine, where I lived for part of this project, but Bangor, Maine; Portsmouth and Manchester, New Hampshire; Haverhill, Newburyport, Lawrence, Salem, Lowell, and Worcester, Massachusetts; and all the suburbs of Boston have their own shelters and soup kitchens, as well as enormous rental prices. Worse, many cities no longer have much or any "affordable housing"; millions of units that had once held boarding houses, single-room occupancy units (SROs) or other housing for low-income people have been destroyed and/or replaced by expensive condominiums or other middle- to upper-class housing (see the National Coalition for the Homeless website, www.nationalhomeless.org, for documentation; on the numbers of housing units lost over the last three decades, see also chapter 3 here). Government policy since the 1980s has been "to get out of the housing business" and beginning with major cuts in the budget of HUD (Housing and Urban Development) has now also included the privatization of public housing[16] and the backlog of the major subsidy program for the poor (Section 8), which means that some cities no longer maintain a waiting list for these programs; the wait goes on for many years.

3. There was a decline in the value and at times even existence of social welfare programs and benefits, with deep cutbacks under President Ronald Reagan and "welfare reform" under President Bill Clinton being among the worst hits. The poor face a different world today than they did in the 1970s; an array of benefits is either no longer available or takes even more hoops to jump through to get than was the case thirty years ago. The decline in Section 8, the close to demise of public housing, the total end of general assistance welfare in some areas (this is often the only aid that a single male or female homeless person is eligible for), the "end of welfare" as applied to AFDC (Aid to Families with Dependent Children) making it a temporary, so-called "jobs" program with strict requirements and strong sanctions are all examples of this trend. AFDC was replaced by TANF (Temporary Assistance to Needy Families) which made "welfare" a non-enti-

tlement with limited time stays and obligations to work (Hays, *Flat Broke with Children* is still one of the best books about the transition from AFDC to TANF).[17] But even where benefits still exist, such as food stamps and unemployment insurance, their value has been weakened by the lack of adjustments in their worth to keep up with inflation. Fewer and fewer people are eligible for unemployment insurance for many reasons including the growth of ineligible part-time, temporary, contingent, consultant, and other "permanent" labor that is not full time. Some states have initiated fees for clients on Medicaid, meaning you must have money to see a doctor or nurse.

4. Though not all experts agree, the deinstitutionalization of mental hospitals and facilities for the developmentally disabled led to a number of former patients being cast out on the streets. Even more important, people in recent years who might have become patients if there were room in institutions did not because the commitment laws have been changed radically. The timing of the deinstitutionalization itself does not fully parallel the homeless crisis. Mental hospitals had been shedding patients since the 1950s when Thorazine was first synthesized. In the older days, former mental patients lived in SRO housing or other cheap units supported by disability checks. It was not so much deinstitutionalization but the first three factors above *combined* with this trend that caused many mentally ill people to become homeless. Thrown out of their apartments by landlords, cut off disability rolls under Reagan (500,000 people were found to have been illegally cut off the rolls in 1981–1984), they had no money or places to live. Courts eventually ruled that cuts in Social Security disability and Supplemental Security Income (SSI) were illegal because of due process violations, but only half those cut off were ever tracked down by advocates (about a quarter of a million were lost, many of them homeless). There is probably still some effect of mental health policy today in that commitment laws have been made tougher (you must be an imminent threat to yourself or others to be committed).

5. Others would add the terrible policy of the "war on drugs," which has devastated the African American and Latino population in major cities and driven a prison and jail population in America to

six times what it was in 1980. Combined with the increased incarceration of the poor, an arrest record makes it nearly impossible to get good housing, and often to get a job. The government has made it impossible to get public housing or even a student loan with a drug record. A pariah class of people without prospects, many who cannot even vote, has been created by a retaliatory society that wants to "be tough on crime" and pledges "zero tolerance" of many behaviors. It is estimated that two-thirds of our prisoners are incarcerated due to the war on drugs. Two recent books on the drug war are Benavie, *Drugs: America's Holy War* and Alexander, *The New Jim Crow: Mass Incarceration in the Age of Colorblindness*.[18]

6. Many citizens, and some experts, cite drug and alcohol abuse, particularly the "crack" cocaine epidemic, as a cause of homelessness, although it is difficult to produce data that supports the idea that there was less drug use in the 1970s than in the 1980s or 1990s. The reverse is actually true; the highest numbers using drugs occurred in the late 1970s.[19] Some, of course, argue that crack cocaine was more available and stronger than other drugs, but literature tends not to bear this out. The fact is that it was targeted in the war on drugs, leading to high rates of incarceration and other problems for its users, which absent the drug war might not have occurred. The same problem exists for alcohol use. We have several issues here. One is that the fact that a homeless person on the street takes a drink does not mean that this was the *cause* of his or her homelessness, and the same goes for drugs. In fact, many homeless people have told me the tremendous stress and tedium of having nothing to do all day but stand in lines or check empty bulletin boards for jobs often facilitate the use of substances on the street. Second, alcoholism and drug use have been around for a long time, yet in the 1940s–1970s era there was little, if any, homelessness.

One can add in many other issues: for example, changes in the family that make it less likely to house certain difficult members, whether adolescents or older people. Importantly, all changes intertwine with one another and homelessness is best seen as *multicausal*. Just as in an earthquake and tsunami, it is usually the poorest in the most vulnerable homes who suffer most, losing jobs or housing. These devastating blows interact with conditions such as alcohol and drug use, domestic violence and child abuse and neglect, and mental illness to pile up problems on those most vulnerable.

Many Americans still prefer to focus on personal and individual issues of homelessness such as mental illness and substance use. They do so less out of ideology, I believe, than out of a lack of understanding of how social structure affects lives. It may make people feel a little better to believe they will never be homeless, ostensibly because they are not drug users or mentally ill. But a thought experiment reveals problems with this line of thinking: the vast majority of mentally ill people, alcoholics, and drug addicts are *not* and *never* were homeless. And if homelessness were tied only to these issues, where were the mentally ill and alcoholics and drug addicts in the 1950s, 1960s, and 1970s? The question answers itself because they had housing. Cheaper available housing, combined with a better economy with more blue-collar jobs, are only two of the conditions that allowed most people to have housing even if they had disabilities.

We have also gained some knowledge about who is likely to be homeless. We do not really have a very sophisticated technology for this and therefore even after thirty-five years our data is contested. Generally though, whether the counters are government census takers or social service providers, the only two types of homeless they count are the sheltered homeless (whose number is relatively easy to ascertain) and some small number of people living outside who are visible to the counters. Likely these numbers are a small fraction of the large numbers staying elsewhere each night, from cars to abandoned buildings to tent cities to couch surfing to doubling up. Moreover, as I will elaborate, each count is only a "point-in-time" count. We can say that someone estimated on January 1, 1990, that there were x number of homeless people, but on January 2, a whole new set of homeless may have appeared, while by February 1, a significant number of those who were homeless on January 1 may be housed. Of our three examples, perhaps no one was counted: Carolyn became homeless January 4; no one came down to the area Mark was staying in, so he was not counted; and neither Paula nor Gabe were counted as they were couch surfing that night. No wonder a city like Portland, Maine, can cite a ridiculous count such as finding four or five non-sheltered people homeless on a given winter night, while in reality there were many more homeless people who were not counted. This process is repeated annually in the homeless counts supervised by the US HUD agency.

It appears that most homeless people are still single men, although a significant minority are women with children or other families. Studies of shelter users and other counted homeless people repeatedly find a high disproportion of African American and Native American people, although this is a little less the case for Latinos.[20] Most homeless people are relatively young, unlike the old "Skid Row" stereotype. They tend to be in their twenties and early thirties rather than older. Of course several factors, including a low life expectancy for the poor and especially homeless people, make long life rare. I have frequently met people on the street who at first glance seemed to be in their sixties and seventies, but often turned out to be far younger. By educational standards, most homeless people are now high school graduates and some have college. The levels are trending upward as more people get more education, yet do not get good jobs.

Whether all this data is accurate may be called into question because of the way we count the homeless (see below). It is possible that more women or families are "hidden" homeless who are "doubled up" in vehicles or abandoned housing or elsewhere. Though somewhat unlikely, it is possible that more whites may be short-term homeless or choose to avoid shelters, and perhaps Latinos are put up more by their families, garages being a major place of shelter by word of mouth in California and the Southwest. Whether there would be any effect on the age or educational backgrounds is unclear. My sense is that although the numbers the government uses are profound underestimates, we do not have proof that gender, age, race, ethnicity, and other descriptors are necessarily incorrect.

THE PERSONAL AND THE BROADER SYSTEM

Mark, described above, provides a perfect example of how the issue of homelessness becomes misinterpreted. Because Mark has developed a drinking problem, he will be categorized by the public if they pass him, and by not a few professionals working in the social service field, as a "typical" alcoholic homeless man. Notice first, no one is probing what occurred *before* he was homeless; an industrial worker with a wife of twelve years with two children, and perhaps a homeowner. Deindustrialization preceded his heavy alcohol use; he is a victim very much of that more than alcoholism. Once Mark is without adequate work, like many people, he becomes edgy, anxious, and depressed. He quarrels with his wife, and later his parents. What options does Mark see in his deserted Midwestern town? Jobs at McDonald's or a hardware or convenience store, which pay minimum wage without benefits, and which he finds degrading, particularly when his friends come in for service. He cannot pay his $600 mortgage, which makes him even more depressed, and he feels less of a provider. Where can he and his wife, and later he, move? He does not have the $800 a month they charge him for a newly completed apartment complex outside of town, and he would also have to come up with a deposit and last month's rent ($2,400 total). He manages for a while at his parents', but he sees few options in his area for his factory skills, and the cheapest rental he has heard of is $550, which would leave him very little to live on even if he uses food stamps, which is the only program he is eligible for.

Homelessness is multicausal because despite the individual circumstances and the personal ways of coping with distress, the broader issues go back to the economy, housing market, and social benefit structure. These, along with other issues at the "macro level" of our society, limit individuals' potential and limit what they can achieve. Can anyone say Mark would be better moving elsewhere? To where? He would miss his children and is not guaranteed a job wherever he goes.

Those who look only at the individual in society fail to account for the major issues in life that most people share, at least that percentage of society that is not making six figures. The necessity of finding decent work has become more difficult, as has finding adequate affordable housing, and supporting oneself with some way of supplementing the income.

THE POLITICS OF HOMELESSNESS

Like most modern social problems, the rediscovery of homelessness as an issue in the 1980s was occasioned by much political fire and partisan clashes. Although homelessness has greatly fallen out of the news in the last twenty years compared to the 1980s and early 1990s,[21] generally it is a cause that liberals and some political radicals championed while conservatives complained that the problem was exaggerated or that blame was misplaced. As with most issues, the public likely stands somewhere in the middle, with compassion toward the most seemingly "deserving" populations (veterans, mothers, and small children) but feelings of disdain toward the very visible homeless, and particularly men and those who appear to be able bodied.

This is not surprising, given that the American history of calling for government intervention to help the homeless came first from the liberal and leftist quarters, with resistance from conservative figures. Ronald Reagan, president when homelessness first became widely recognized, himself made light of the issue and even questioned why people went to soup kitchens, suggesting that they enjoyed the food.[22] In turn, opponents charged with some success that the administration was "heartless" and "unfeeling," and many encampments used names like "Reaganville" or "Reagan City" to label their tent cities. Among the most famous of advocates was Mitch Snyder, once a business executive, who quit his job to work with the CCNV (Coalition for Creative Non-Violence) which picked up the issue in the late 1970s. By the mid-1980s, Snyder went on frequent hunger strikes to bring attention to the homeless issue and led many militant protests. Somewhat less well known, attorney Robert Hayes quit a corporate job to develop the Coalition for the Homeless, and among other things successfully sued the City of New York and obtained a consent decree that forced New York City to house the homeless in shelters. Despite a great deal of protest that often called for strong remediation and social justice, government at the local level decided to emphasize homeless shelters, soup kitchens, clothes closets, and other charitable aid in the 1980s. The first and only major federal governmental act, the Stewart McKinney Act of 1987, primarily calls for federal aid to shelters and services, with less emphasis on the search for permanent housing, much less jobs and income as some radicals and liberals called for.

Over time, neither the liberal side nor conservative opponents have been all that "liberal" or all that "conservative" in action. Although there are still some radical groups engaged in poverty and homeless work, homeless advocates and workers are generally liberal, and while good, compassionate people, they very rarely see beyond the social services they themselves provide, at least in a systematic way, to demand changes that might *end* homelessness. Similarly, just as Eisenhower's election saw the Republicans get used to Social Security and other welfare state benefits, the Bush administration with "its kinder, gentler" conservatism was accepting of the ameliorative policies toward the homeless, and George W. Bush aimed programs at the goal of eliminating "chronic homelessness." Of course, funding never appeared to actually come along with these goals.

My interest here is how the politicization makes actual factual descriptive presentations difficult. Homelessness is an extreme form of poverty that was not new in the 1980s, but has characterized American history from the time when old village settlements threw "vagabonds" and "vagrants" out of town.[23] In a sense, the political separation of a "homeless population" (much less a homeless mentally ill population, a homeless veteran population, and so on) are *reifications* of people who usually start out fairly poor and who much of the time will go back into housing, but still remain poor. While certainly there are still some conservatives who view homeless people as deviants (special forms of population because something is wrong with them) and not a few liberals who agree but urge compassion to the vulnerable, the issue is no longer a clear liberal/conservative one. It is not just that we lack the Mitch Snyders and Robert Hayeses of the 1980s, but the fact that neither political party has even the remotest agenda to end homelessness or long-term poverty because to do so would take eroding of social trends that have been ongoing for four decades and would take a considerable investment of money (and probably power redistribution) to achieve. Issues of jobs for all, housing for all, income for those disabled or out of work, while guaranteed in the United Nations Declaration of Human Rights, are just not on the US agenda. These issues have certainly been pressed by some on the left, and what remains of a homeless movement; see the films of the Poor People's Economic and Human Rights Coalition (PPEHRC), *Outriders* and *Living Broke in Boom Times*[24] and recently the film *More Than a Roof* showing the visit of the UN Rapporteur criticizing America's treatment of the homeless.[25] No politician on the left, center, or right discusses poverty or homelessness, but rather only addresses the "middle class."

A NEW STRATEGY: LOOKING AT THE
FORMERLY HOMELESS

A major contradiction develops with our way of counting and to some extent conceptualizing homelessness. Whether we count the hundreds of thousands of people a night homeless or several million as advocates tend to say, the vast undercount of homelessness as well as the "floating" nature of the population (in time and space) means that those who study the general citizenry find far more millions of people saying they have been homeless than any "point-in-time" study has found. That is, more people have been homeless than come to the official attention of media or academics, and the gap is one of many millions of people.

What this suggests, and this book will focus on, is that a study of the ex-homeless may be more accurate and interesting in the twenty-first century than a study of those who are homeless on a given day. There is both a logical and more philosophical statement here. It is logical in that if as many as thirty million people have been homeless at some point in time in, say, the last five years, why focus on only the small number of "long-term homeless" or even the homeless present on one day?

But there are major philosophical issues hidden within the logical statement. Should we confine the study of homelessness to people who are often stereotyped as "homeless" (i.e., long-term homeless who are visible at the corners or the lines of shelters and soup kitchens)? Many on both sides of the political spectrum may at times argue "yes." The George W. Bush (and then Obama) initiative on "chronic homelessness" was based on the idea that these longer-term homeless cost the service, health, and governmental systems far more money than the short-term homeless, and therefore should be prioritized. People on the left or at least liberal side of the spectrum, so influential in raising the problem of homelessness to begin with, may with some cause call us out for abandoning the most difficult and needy people if we emphasize, say, the short-term homeless.

The argument (or perhaps better framed as the *Rashomon*-like nature of the problem) is akin to how to characterize "mentally ill" people and their needs. Many average citizens conceptualize the term *mental illness* as a scary and aggressive state of an actively psychotic person (hearing voices, screaming, threatening people). Yet many other Americans who take antidepressants and other pharmaceuticals will protest with great emotion that actually the majority of people with "mental illness" function daily in our society and should arouse no major fears. The very "worst" face of the problem (psychotic behavior) is often folded into the many cases of mild disorders. We do not have appropriate language to separate them, and this is the case too with homelessness.

Interestingly in the case of mental illness, advocates and experts have tended to rather self-interestedly hold on to the broader, expansive definition of "mental health" and "mental illness" such that declarations are made constantly that something on the order of one in four Americans will suffer a mental illness. These dramatic numbers, as Horwitz suggests,[26] are obtained by taking the maximum number of complaints about depression and other problems, and expanding these issues over a lifetime prevalence (e.g., if you said you were depressed to a survey researcher, you will be counted as mentally troubled, though in a few days you may have felt better, and, in any case, you never consulted a mental health practitioner).

This book does not suggest that we take such an expansive view of homelessness, which results in an overstated view. In fact, I have criticized the earlier mantra of some homeless advocates that "anyone can become homeless."[27] Rather, it seems that as experts and advocates approach a richer and truer portrait of the homeless, they need to include the many people who tend to be shorter-term homeless, less involved in shelters and services, and possibly even more diverse than the groups frequently studied. In other words, I am by no means calling for an exaggeration or inflation of the numbers of homeless people, but rather seek a focus on the more common short-term and episodic nature of homelessness for many millions of poor people.

For three interlinked reasons, this book explores the *ex-homeless* because

1. It provides a continual reminder that for most people homelessness is not the end of the road of life, but only a step on the road. Like jail and prison, most people do get out.
2. Students of homelessness, when they talk to the homeless, if they do at all, do so only at the point when they are the most vulnerable, entering a shelter, for example, or living in a public area. The comments of these people are not without value, but we

must recognize that they are shaped by the extreme vulnerability and marginalization they feel, not a long-thought-out position or an analysis that might come in a deeper interview in a more comfortable setting.

3. Because of the focus on the most visible homeless in media and academia, and mostly on shelter or other service users, ex-homeless studies provide a far broader picture of the types of people who were homeless with a broader range of opinion and experiences.

So far, although there have been academic articles on formerly homeless people, generally these individuals are treated as an experimental group to see if a certain program or service has "succeeded." The studies almost all lack generalizability because they are focused on a small segment of the homeless—such as "co-occurring disorders" (drugs and mental illness), the elderly, veterans, youth, etc.—in a particular setting.[28] Although understandable in terms of resources for research, in reality in most communities these groups are not isolated by themselves, but live in the community with other people. The most simple and profound statements come from an early study by Mary Beth Shinn and associates,[29] which found that no variable had an influence on housing success except the provision of a housing subsidy! Similarly, the Department of Housing and Urban Development recently arrived at the same conclusions even when comparing their own programs for the homeless.[30] I believe the formerly homeless can teach us more than this, however, both to observe them in a more holistic way, to find out what types of lives they lead (which is impossible to really ascertain without visiting them in their communities and asking them), and also in talking with them about their experiences being homeless and becoming housed. While it is true that my sample is hardly large enough to speak for the entire population of ex-homeless (see below), it is large enough to cover many types of formerly homeless people by geography, race and ethnicity, and various statuses (age, gender, mental illness, substance use, etc.).

AN EXAMPLE OF THE LARGE SIZE AND FLUIDITY OF A HOMELESS POPULATION

It is very hard for most people to fully understand large numbers and complex statistics, such as the scope of homelessness in the country as a whole. For this reason, the ebb and flow of homeless people into and out of a single shelter may be easier schematically to understand. We take for simplicity's sake a shelter that has 100 beds—in this day and age, probably inadequate except for a small city or a large town. In the example in table 1.1, we say the shelter is full on January 1 (seasonal variations are common in shelter use, but not always in the direction people perceive; some local shelters in Maine, for example, are more filled in the summer, presumably because there is a higher transient or visitor population).

When we look at the same shelter on July 1, it is slightly less than full (ninety-three people). However, as is common, only a certain number are the same individuals; in this example I have used thirty-three, but this is not a scientific number. Much depends on the perceived quality of the shelter, the season and weather, the employment and housing markets, and many other factors including deaths and people who simply move away. Even where some shelters attempt to keep track of homeless individuals, they rarely do so in a long-term manner. A man may say he is going to Idaho, but does not; an ill man says he is checking into a clinic, but does not and dies; a man promised work does not get it

Table 1.1.   A Representation of Number of People Moving In and Out of a Homeless Shelter

Date	Numbers
Shelter Population January 1, 2014	100
Shelter Population July 1, 2014	93
Same person	33
New admissions still present	45
Readmissions from previous years	15
Total new admissions January 1–July 1, 2014	(489)
Total return admissions January 1–July 1, 2014	(234)
Total individuals	756

and moves in with his family; a woman who says she is moving in with family does not, but is sleeping outside now that the weather is warm. There are many possible permutations.

Looking at the shelter on July 1, we have thirty-three of the same people, and assuming that the shelter keeps some rudimentary records, we see that forty-five homeless people are new admissions in the last few weeks, while fifteen people have been previous visitors. But the real record of discrete different individuals is far higher: from January 1 to July 1, 489 new homeless people were admitted (with most leaving) and 234 people with previous stays at the shelter have come in (and many out). The hundred-bed shelter held 756 different individuals between January and July 2.[31]

The example is meant not only to illustrate the large numbers of people who come through a homeless shelter, but the variety of reasons for departure: again, they range from death to incarceration, to employment to stays with friends and relatives, to obtaining housing, to leaving town, to mention only a few. Further, of all the sites where homeless people stay in our little city, the shelter is the most organized. Homeless people who stay in others' apartments, in "squats" or other makeshift arrangements, in cars, abandoned buildings, and so on are not adequately counted to begin with, much less is there any longitudinal documentation about them. Those who escape the very limited counting agencies of our service system over time are lost to information seekers as they fend by themselves for better or worse.

But even if we had the best records scholars might want, the number of people living in makeshift arrangements, others' homes, semi-institutions (jails, group homes, and halfway houses), cars, garages, and such must be observed daily to examine the flow in and out from one to another. These numbers then must be compared with death records and incarceration rates to name only some of the factors to trace the homeless. Hence a city of 30,000, for example, might have 1,500 homeless people although its shelter houses only 100, and could have a flow of perhaps 3,000 people a year in and out of shelters and other places for the homeless. The above examples suggest some of the difficulty in studying the homeless at one point in time and the even harder problem of finding those who have been homeless.

PURPOSE OF THIS BOOK

This book broadly attempts to do two main things: one is to destigmatize people with the awful label of "homeless" (and the worse ones often informally thrown at them such as "bums," "tramps," and so on) by seeing who the homeless really are and what some of them are capable of achieving once housed in the community. Naturally, it is likely that the reader is more sympathetic to people who are poor than the average American. When one seeks to destigmatize a despised group, it is very difficult to reach the audience that are often the most intolerant. One has to hope that those who read and understand can communicate as individuals to their communities, friends, neighbors, and even political leaders that something is wrong in America when so many people are poor or homeless, and the situation is worsening with the years.

I write as someone who has had the privilege of seeing people change over the years, of having had former homeless people in his university classes, and of seeing people who were once homeless lead meetings and rallies and other organized activities in several cities. I have seen some people who were addicted become non-addicted. I have seen people with mental health problems improve. I have also been impressed by many people who still have severe mental health problems and how much they can do (see my profile of "Amy").[32]

I claim no special qualities for having witnessed this. Partly I have lived in a relatively small city where it is easy to observe people, and I have a rather good memory for names and faces, and recognize people. But I do not think this makes me or the people I describe exceptional. Similarly through contacts, I have observed some people engaged in community organizing and political action from the lowest socioeconomic parts of our society, and seen a great deal of sophistication and wisdom from them. Again, these groups are out there and can be observed, but they rarely have middle-class visitors other than grant funders or social service providers.

By making some of these stories public, I hope that the damning labels that accompany so many people who are poor can be partly removed, though I know this is a tall order. My book presents some "success stories," both success as defined in a mainstream way such as graduating from university or securing a good job, but also in what constitutes reasonable success at the bottom level of society. Given the conditions in our nation for those who are in the poverty population, I feel strongly that formerly homeless people who have gained some housing security or income or employment security need to be seen as "successes" as well. Many of the people profiled in chapters 2–6 have been successful as organizational and community actors, involved in art, self-help and recovery groups, and political and religious groups, to name a few. The success of community life as well as friendships and partners is at least as important as success in the work field.

More specifically, the book draws on fifty-one in-depth interviews with formerly homeless people, some of whom I know in northern New England and Southern California, and some of whom I do not know but found through "snowball" samples of contacts in California, New England, and Washington, DC. I have tried to shape my interview sample by the demographic material available on the adult homeless population, although as I have mentioned, there is some controversy as to whether we have good numbers.

In addition to working to destigmatize the homeless label, in this book I aim to offer evidence in support of changing how research funds are used to investigate what seem to be the same approaches to homeless and poverty research. Our research institutions, funders, and those who receive funds are fairly resistant to change, and often research the same thing in the same way over and over. But as I indicated earlier, there are many weaknesses to the research on homelessness, and leaders of national advocacy groups agree that we need studies of the ex-homeless to better understand outcomes of homelessness and to get a more complete story about homelessness. Only by seeing the stigmatizing terms of homelessness and poverty as steps and places along a lifetime can we get a sense of the fluidity of life, and for that matter, the many people who experience these conditions.

I hope to open an avenue that uses the terms "ex-homeless" and "formerly homeless" to be a research category at least at this time because it may elucidate how many poor people and others have found themselves homeless, how people have managed to overcome this experience, and the light they can shed to others about what it is like, to be both homeless and housed.

Although my study is small in the sense of interviewing fifty-one people, it combines people from sites as diverse as "Skid Row" Los Angeles and Washington, DC, to small city, suburban, and rural Maine,

New Hampshire, and Massachusetts. Using the latest demographic figures we have, the sample is similar in gender, single or family status,
and race and ethnicity to national samples. There are some areas, as
further discussed in appendix I, in which the formerly homeless cannot
be expected to resemble the current homeless. The people I interviewed ranged from recently housed to those housed for as long as
twenty years. Not surprisingly, the people I interviewed are older, and
at least a bit more educated and involved in work than current homeless
people. Please see appendix I for the reasoning behind the study, the
approach and questions asked, and the demographics of the people
interviewed.

2

PROFILES OF FORMERLY HOMELESS PEOPLE

Some Surprising Successes

GLIMPSES OF THE EX-HOMELESS

Because of the societal prejudice against homeless people, my first order of business is to show how very "normal" these people are. Many have said that the homeless are "just like you or me"—they shared the same humanity with the strengths and frailties we all have. But both the circumstances and appearance of the ex-homeless obviously have changed considerably since they were homeless, to a point where the people profiled here are no longer as vulnerable; nor do they appear as different as they once might have. Moreover, the environments of the people I interviewed and visited seem quite different from those of people I have met who are homeless. While homeless people vary considerably in their attire, hygiene and grooming, articulateness, and all other dimensions, still there was quite a difference between visiting a former homeless person (some who had not been homeless for many years) and meeting people while they are living on the street or at a shelter. I was surprised at what a difference this made.

Quite often I had to remind myself that the person I was interviewing had been homeless, and in a few interviews, I was concerned at first that I had the wrong person or that the information was conveyed incorrectly to the subject, who had not been homeless (or perhaps had been for only a very short time).[1] Obviously the factors of having a roof over one's head and in most cases an income that at least afforded food, clothes, and other minimal necessities make quite a difference in a person's life.

I did not visit the apartments of all those I interviewed, but in New England at least some of the new digs of the ex-homeless that I did visit seemed surprisingly nice. For example, when I visited Ian (profiled later in the chapter) a man who was on the streets for many years but had overcome a severe and life-threatening alcohol addiction, I was surprised when I got to the address to see a brick façade building modeled after historical preservation areas of Portland, Maine. His one-bedroom apartment had recently refinished hardwood floors. It turned out to have been renovated some years before by a nonprofit organization. Similarly, I drove to Sandy's (profiled later in the chapter) home in the fairly tony town of Amesbury, Massachusetts, just across the border with New Hampshire. Sandy is a man in his late fifties with two children who was homeless after his disability check from the federal government was cut off. Although his house rental was certainly not in the fanciest part of town, still it was a suburban setting with adequate yard and space inside for the children, one a teen and one a special needs child of eleven. Again, I found myself a little unsure of quite where I was until Sandy answered my question of how he became homeless in detail. Interestingly, Sandy received his house (for rent) from the Haverhill, Massachusetts–based nonprofit organization Emmaus Inc. through a raffle there; he confided in me that he has never been sure if he actually won the raffle or if some staff member had taken pity on him with his two children, and somehow altered the drawing in his favor.

I do not mean to overstate this. There are clearly formerly homeless people who are in slum housing with poor conditions and, as I will discuss, many people have episodic homelessness that propels them in and out of housing. The people referred to me were often (though not always) those who had reached a level of stability. Also in some cases, the homeless may have benefited somewhat from nonprofit agencies' scrutiny of the housing before it was offered to them. In Los Angeles I did not visit apartments because it was far easier and more convenient to use the offices of the centrally located Los Angeles Community Action Network (LACAN) on East Sixth Street for interviews rather than go to each subject's apartment. Since some subjects, though not the majority, lived in single room occupancy (SRO) hotels or boarding houses, their digs would have been quite different from the examples above.

Nevertheless, I offer these descriptions as "success stories" of ex-homelessness. I have taken some time to describe more than a few (over twenty) of my subjects because I think the reader will be surprised by how accomplished these people are. And by "accomplishment," I do not mean just success in gaining an educational degree or some form of employment, but success in living, in becoming not only rehoused, but part of a community, and by being able to be productive people through activities and passions.[2] In a sense, I use the word "success" to indicate a concept that Erik Erikson called "generativity," although he used the word for seniors.[3] But in a society in which former homeless people for the most part will have difficulty finding interesting (if any) jobs, generativity must include the ability to be community members and to have their skills used in various forms of art, service, or avocations.

For convenience I have organized the discussion about these subjects into different categories: former students of mine who were once homeless, social service workers who were homeless and homeless people who then became service workers, artists who were homeless or homeless people who became artists when housed, former homeless people who are now advocates for their fellow homeless and others, and a number of people whose persistence against the odds seemed incredible to me. Obviously there is some subjectivity here, but it is important to share stories of people who have overcome homelessness in the fashion these people have.

FORMERLY HOMELESS PEOPLE GETTING COLLEGE DEGREES

To my knowledge, there is no data kept on either college students who were once homeless or people who are actually homeless when they go to college. Anecdotally, state universities and community colleges, if not private universities, have more than a few students who are or became homeless over the years attending college (now more likely to be eight or nine years than four). It is likely that people who were formerly homeless and are now housed are not at all unusual students in many of our colleges (as I was writing, a report from California State Universities, the largest state system in the nation, found that 10 percent of their students may have been homeless;[4] see also a study at California State University at Long Beach for a similar finding).[5]

At two schools where I have taught (both attended by working-class and some poor students) informal surveys I have taken reveal high numbers of formerly homeless students. In one class of mine at the University of Southern Maine in Portland, seven of the seventeen students said they had been homeless at some point in their lives. In a class I gave in homelessness at California State University at Dominguez Hills in Carson, California (CSUDH), seven of the twenty-one students revealed they were formerly homeless. There is no way of telling if there were still others who had been homeless and did not say. Definitional questions also always plague such surveys or discussions.

Whether the actual number is 15 percent, 10 percent, or 6 percent of students, the following three people are only a few of many of the people I have met on both coasts who had been homeless and were now attending or graduating from college.

Bob, a sixty-year-old man I met when he took a class in homelessness I gave at the University of Southern Maine, was quite cautious about revealing his background. I have found this common, because even in a field such as social work many students have stereotypes and misconceptions about homeless people. Moreover, even if not, a revelation about oneself runs the risk of feeling that you will be made a spokesperson for a group, just as sometimes minority students feel that they are in this role. As the course went on, it became clear that Bob knew a great deal about homelessness, and something in his appearance and mannerism suggested to me he might have been homeless (he had a deeply furrowed face and brow that seemed prematurely old, for example). Late in the class, Bob asked me if I would mind reading something he had written for an English class. I agreed and found that I thoroughly enjoyed his short story about two homeless men on the streets. It became quite clear to me without Bob ever saying so that indeed he had been homeless somewhere in the general area.

Bob was happy to get together to be interviewed. He had just graduated with his bachelor's degree, and was looking forward to earning his master's degree. He suggested that we meet at an upscale coffee house in Portland, with deeply cushioned, comfortable seats with which he was obviously familiar. He was already sitting where he wished when I came in, and we decided we were both comfortable there. After some preliminaries, Bob went into his life story, which required few interruptions for clarification or comment; he clearly had done this before.

Bob was from a fairly typical working-class family in nearby Windham, a town about fifteen miles north of Portland. Most of his life until his late thirties resembled others, although some discussion of family issues growing up prefigured some personal problems. In his late thirties, two things happened: one was that a job he had worked at and enjoyed for years at a wastewater facility in the city of Saco, Maine (about ten miles south of Portland), became "horrible" as a supervisor appointed through nepotism "had it in" for Bob and began harassing him. Meanwhile, his marriage of a decade and a half began to falter. The stress began to lead him to drink more. His divorce was relatively amicable and he continued to see his two young children. But his drinking increased even more when he got a job with a stone working company and lived on the road in motels. "Now I could drink whenever I want[ed]," chuckled Bob. He also noted the connection between his not getting a home, but simply staying in hotels as his work kept him out of state. "It was really the beginning of my homelessness." Indeed, in an interesting phenomenon I have seen, Bob went from staying in hotels to staying in his vehicle, to finally having to stay in the streets and forests.

Although he was homeless for three years, he considers himself relatively lucky, compared to many men who hang out in Portland who are "street drunks." He was not literally homeless (that is, on the streets as compared to in housing) for a long time, and he kept in some touch with his family. His sister had told him that if he was ever ready to go to the detoxification unit at a local hospital to call her, and when he did, she immediately drove him there. It was a long way coming back, including a two-year stay at a group home for former alcoholics where the men paid the rent and did all the chores. He credits a therapist for helping him a great deal over the years, including getting him subsidized housing, and he is happy that he "found he liked school so much, it has been fun."

Debbie, fifty-seven, and Violet, forty-one, were two of the students I had at California State–Dominguez Hills (they are both graduating now) when I taught a class in the Sociology Department. Debbie was a very quiet student, but when she spoke she was nearly always on target; Violet was more active and contributed quite a bit to the class; sometimes one could tell that she was a little frustrated by misconceptions about poverty that other students had. Debbie's history resembles Bob's to some extent, although she was born in Honduras. Her early decades were unremarkable and after graduating from high school she worked for a decade at the *Los Angeles Times* newspaper. In her early thirties, she married and had two children. Unfortunately, her husband was hitting the bottle harder and harder, and she began abusing drugs. She had already gone through rehabilitation and a twelve-step program, but after having dental work, she became addicted to pain killers. The combination of her and her husband's substance abuse and splitting up led Debbie onto the streets, although her in-laws were able to take her children so she did not have to have them with her on the streets.

She was literally homeless for a year and a half, at first "couch surfing" with friends and relatives, then living out of vehicles, and finally in homeless shelters. The family had moved to the desert town of Victorville, California, and she found the community extremely hostile to homeless people. She worked her way down to the South Bay area (between Long Beach and Los Angeles) where she found extremely mixed reactions—for example, the police in Torrance threatened her never to return there—but other towns were more tolerant.

The turning point for Debbie was her acceptance into a rehabilitation program of the Harbor Interfaith Family Shelter (in Harbor City, California), which provided a sober living program. She has a great deal of praise for this program, which unusually provided not only housing but income support while she returned to school. At this point she had her children back and was receiving AFDC (Aid to Families with Dependent Children). Neither she nor her two oldest children will forget the experiences of that time. And Debbie, faced with the high rents and prices of California, was not totally sanguine about her future. She currently lives on disability benefits, which just about cover only her rent. Her children, two now in their twenties, help her out, and "without that," she said, "I would probably be homeless still." Nevertheless, she is interested in applying for a master's degree program in social work.

As Debbie was now housed for fourteen years, my former student Violet has been housed for seventeen. While obviously discussions of homelessness will not be as raw as those who were homeless more recently, the rarity of hearing the stories of formerly homeless people who are now stable makes these experiences worth sharing.

Violet, in fact, owns her own home in Compton, California. Violet describes herself as a rebellious child who was something of a trouble-maker. She married at seventeen when she became pregnant and she "was extremely immature in a lot of ways." She was able to stay with her mother at first, but then after a miscarriage, she became pregnant again. The father was abusive, and she lost a job at a movie theater because the manager would not put up with her boyfriend's violent outbursts. After that, she could not go home and she became homeless in 1995. She lived with relatives for a while, but this didn't work as she could get no sleep; the room she and the child stayed in was constantly invaded by other people. In 1996–1997 she lived out of a van on the streets of Long Beach, California. Violet noted that "she always worked" and was doing a gig as a security guard at the time. Violet, like many homeless and formerly homeless people I have interviewed, never went into the "system" of shelters or services for the homeless. Her pride was clearly too great. Surprisingly, she had little trouble with authorities; she knew "how to lean down in the van to not be seen" and which streets she could get away with parking in.

Over the last decades, Violet pulled herself up educationally, starting at Long Beach City College, getting an associate's degree at Cerritos College, and then transferring to California State University. She also has worked for many years as a paralegal, giving her a secure income. Like Bob and Debbie, Violet is anxious to go to graduate school, looking at psychology and criminal justice programs.

MOVING FROM CLIENT TO WORKER AND BACK IN THE SOCIAL SERVICES

Although perhaps not well known to the public, most counselors, social workers, and other related professionals are aware that a major vehicle for upward movement from poverty or even working-class status to the middle class has been working in the social services themselves. The "War on Poverty" programs made this an explicit goal, so that what were called in the old days "paraprofessionals" would be trained people from the poorer communities who could achieve upward mobility in jobs with titles such as case aides, mental hygiene therapists, recreational assistants, legal assistants, and so on. Although helping people who have experienced social problems into social service professions has hardly been a political goal in recent years, a large number of students in the human service professions come from lower classes and often have experienced the very social problems they now work to alleviate.

But given that social service workers themselves, even those with college and graduate degrees, do not make that much money, and often come into their professions through empathy with people based on their own lives, it is not surprising that as well as upward mobility, there are numbers of social service workers who also become downwardly mobile.

The profiles present us with mobility in both directions. Cass, now a community organizer on Los Angeles's Skid Row and also an activist in many political and community endeavors there, is a man who had a great deal of education and intellect, but also a substance abuse problem that helped propel him into homelessness. Another formerly homeless woman named Shirley suffered domestic violence and over the years came to be an activist with Los Angeles's Downtown Women's Advocacy Center (DWAC), and the Los Angeles Community Action Network (LACAN).

Cass, sixty-four, admits that he lived a kind of strange "double life." He was a very well-educated person who got a degree at City College in New York in a public-service oriented joint degree in legal studies, and passed the bar exam in New York. But in each period of his life he jokes about how he also had an active street life and drug life. I got my "GED at the Brooklyn House of Detention," he jokes, and was not in Vietnam but in the "war across 110th Street" (in Morningside Heights-Manhattan Valley, New York City). Cass's story, while filled with humor, had its sad points, including his disbarment from the law for selling drugs. He says "his large ego" enabled him to justify being at once a street hustler and also a prominent professional. Then after his rehabilitation succeeded in 2002 he has pledged to give back to his community, Skid Row in Los Angeles, so that so many people, particularly black men like himself, need not go through what he has gone through.

In contrast to Cass, Fara, forty-four, a tall and striking woman born in Guyana, became a counselor in Massachusetts where she obtained not only a college degree but a master's degree and was working on an online PhD. However, nearly two years ago, a series of difficult circumstances led to Fara becoming homeless. A health problem (she needed a double knee replacement) led her to essentially being fired from her social service job when she could not return to work in a timely way. Because she needed help recuperating, she moved into her daughter's house in Boston. However, her daughter had just married, and her new son-in-law was not at all happy with the idea of Fara moving in. One thing led to another, and eventually Fara moved out and started living out of her car in the streets of Haverhill, Massachusetts. Her recounting of having to ask for help from the very same organizations she once referred people to or consulted with as a professional was heart rending. Yet Fara was surprisingly philosophical at times about her period of homelessness: "I learned a lot about how people feel and how they handle the issues I thought I knew so much about. In that way it was good."

ARTISTS AND HOMELESSNESS

Just as with the social services, there is a two-way street that links the arts and homelessness. Again, one connection is poverty. There were quite a few people in Los Angeles's Skid Row, for example, who came to Los Angeles hoping to "make it" in film, acting, music, and related industries. Many would be disappointed, and some would actually end up in poverty when something went wrong with their health or they lost a job or a relationship. Another link is that even if a person is not a practicing artist, musician, dancer, or other artist before, art is not an uncommon road back for people who are in the social services and/or rehabilitation; art helps change their lives. While we have no guesses on the percentage of people who engage in artistic activities, there are certainly a fair number who do, some for money and some not. Almost all organizations who work with groups such as homeless people or people with psychiatric problems, for example, have found photography, painting, crafts, writing skills, and other hands-on art genres are tremendously popular and common among people served.

"TRO" is a stage name for a Los Angeles actor. He provides a good example of this direction of homelessness and the arts. He came to the West Coast from New York City years ago at the bidding of his acting friends, who told him "everything is happening" in Los Angeles. TRO was persuaded, but found the first irony was that most of the friends he had in LA had left by several years later. Meanwhile, to support himself, TRO ran a catering business, initially extremely successful. His business worked with some of the larger Hollywood-area companies in serving large parties. However, what goes up, comes down, and the downturn in the economy that hit California particularly hard around 2008–2010 led to his business drying up. Meanwhile, his apartment in downtown Los Angeles, which was comfortable and had a reasonable rent, was hit by the gentrification that has been a major factor in causing homelessness. As the drive to move the building from rentals to condominiums intensified, the landlord began to stop making any repairs to the building. TRO stated that he was "driven out. . . . There was no way to stay as the building . . . was getting dangerous and deteriorating rapidly." In his late fifties, TRO became homeless for the first time in his life. He interestingly described with some bitterness how the social agencies in Skid Row rejected him because he looked so middle class and even had a smartphone.

Another link between some people who were homeless and the arts is that different types of artistic activities are a frequent part of services and rehabilitation. I am not sure of all the links; is it that art as one avenue of independent existence outside the corporate office attracts people with free spirits? Is there something the arts shares in common with some elements of poverty and homelessness that again perhaps includes a rejection of everyday norms?

Two formerly homeless people who were not previously artists exemplify this second direction. Ian is a man in his late fifties who spent most of his life as a self-admitted "drunk," so terribly addicted that he was given up as being "terminal." When Ian turned his life around only four or five years ago, he found that he suddenly loved painting. When I visited Ian in his apartment in Portland, Maine, every square inch (including his bed) was covered with painted canvasses, all very bright and colorful. He could not explain this transformation; he never had painting lessons or classes. Somehow his new energy had moved to art as a means of expression, and the positive feedback by way of sales and mural commissions had obviously encouraged it.

Wally, a middle-aged African American man with an extremely interesting past including education in linguistics and neuro-linguistics (holding a BA and MA respectively), and a four-year stint in the military in a secret unit deployed overseas, had become homeless only after a freak accident that almost took his life. He spent many years bedridden after the collapse of a swimming pool he was repairing led to him becoming paralyzed from the neck down. His "miraculous recovery," as people called it, came at the expense of all his money, his friends, and his girlfriend. When he finally got housing in Los Angeles's Skid Row, Wally, in addition to finally receiving a veteran's pension, became active in several artistic pursuits: theater as a staff member of LAPD (the Los Angeles Poverty Department, an avant-garde theater group based in Skid Row) and as a musician in the "Skid Row Players" group. While Wally was able to discuss more of the roots of his interests than Ian above, there was naturalness about these activities for Wally, who believes the arts plays a huge part in both Skid Row's own culture and that of African Americans. His fascination years ago, for example, with linguistics and cognition brought him back to the roots of drums in the human evolution of art.

FORMER HOMELESS PEOPLE SERVING AS ADVOCATES

Those not involved in the social services may be surprised at how many types of services now either employ (although sometimes on a small stipend) or use as volunteers people who themselves have undergone the condition that is being assisted. Although not standardized, services for substance use (through the original AA and then NA models), mental health, physical disabilities, domestic violence, and HIV/AIDS (as well as homelessness and poverty) are all examples of fields in which people with the condition have played a prominent role. Those areas that are short of funds and have involved political debate or agitation (one thinks of disability rights, AIDS, and domestic violence as well as homelessness) have particularly drawn on the use of people who were often activists themselves in regard to the issue.

Of course, many advocates who are employed or affiliated with non-profit or public organizations do not usually perform the same work as a paid professional in the area. Usually advocates, unless they secure an advanced degree, are more active in areas such as linking people to services or being active in group advocacy on an issue, or are active speakers about an issue to all sorts of other civic organizations, schools, or the media and public. They could not do therapy or substance use treatment, nor could they on their own usually arrange for the acquisition of housing or social benefits such as welfare or Social Security, although they often give good hints of how to act with professionals charged with screening eligibility.

Yet although most advocates I met were affiliated with particular organizations, such as the Los Angeles Community Action Network or the National Coalition for the Homeless, for example, an advocate may also be somewhat self-standing. I reported in my 1993 book on a number of active advocates in "North City."[6] At that time I interviewed my (by now) friend Theodore about his history of homelessness. Theodore has been doing advocacy work for nearly his entire adult life. Theodore is forty-eight now, but goes back to the "tent city" protest reported on in my book, which occurred in Portland (or "North City") in 1987. Theodore, then a young man who had just become homeless, became very entranced with the well-known Mitch Snyder, who was in contact with the protestors. He also met a man named Bob who for many years was an active advocate/organizer for a small group in Maine that came out of the welfare rights movement. Despite being homeless twice himself in the last ten years, Theodore has continued his advocacy work. At his home, he has large files containing information about federal, state, and local benefits and rules, and over the years has attended hearings at the state legislature in Augusta and at the city council in Portland. Theodore even has a radio frequency band that provides him with police and fire information. Theodore has tried in recent years, after Bob passed away, to revive the old welfare rights group, but the meetings have been attended poorly.

Theodore seems to enjoy helping people and also the battle of wits with various organizations and local or state agencies. He seems to have been able to do this in spite of lacking a broader organization or at many points a broader movement in Portland among either the homeless or the poor. To my mind, Theodore seems to have much better coping skills than in years past. He identifies his main difficulty as a mental health problem, some of it stemming from an abusive childhood. Indeed, he was able to get into a much-desired housing project because he was re-diagnosed with Posttraumatic Stress Disorder (PTSD), a relatively new diagnosis for non-veterans with problems not war related. Because he is well connected to service agencies, a psychiatric reevaluation changed his prior diagnoses to PTSD and enabled him to live in a building for disabled and senior people associated with the Catholic Archdiocese of Maine. However, Theodore, like Elliot, another formerly homeless man in Portland I have known for nearly a quarter of a century, was reluctant to fault any of his prior actions or question the time he was homeless. "I'm older now and I can't stay on the streets the way I used to," he says, referencing in particular his near blindness. "Also I have this girlfriend now and we want to get married." Elliot similarly cited age and family plans as central in leaving the streets. But both were protective of their experiences as homeless people, with Elliot stating, "I can survive anywhere on the street or not!"

Jason, another homeless advocate in Portland, presents a very different profile in both his background and his work as an advocate. Although Theodore went to an adoptive family who were not poor, he left early, and was soon thrust out of the Maine Center for the Blind where he lived; he generally has always known poverty. Jason is from a family where his father was a union electrician; he followed him in this line of work. He worked as a master electrician for a long time before he and his coworkers could no longer cover up a growing drinking problem. I have observed him when he was involved with a number of groups, some liberal and some on the Left, such as Occupy! when it was active a few years ago. Despite this, Jason's advocacy work is very circumscribed by the organization that pays him a small stipend to assist homeless and other clients (Portland's largest organization for the very poor). He admits that the small number of advocates cannot exactly do what they want. For example, last year when a prohibition on panhandling was in the process of being enacted I was surprised that neither the larger organization nor its advocacy group supported the opposition to the ban in which other advocates of civil liberties, poverty, and homeless rights were active.

Jason's group is known as the "Homeless Voices for Justice"; the name is somewhat of a misnomer since no member is actually homeless currently. The group, like Theodore, is very capable on day-to-day issues of concern such as the shelter system, helping consumers with problems linking to organizations, and helping people familiarize themselves with benefits. On a day-to-day basis, Jason's work is probably similar to Theodore's in that he assists the newly homeless or others in advice and informal counseling and refers them to others when needed. There is no question that for all advocates, their connections with agencies and services make their lives better. Jason tells a story about how some years ago "he kind of disappeared," drifting back to drinking. A social worker who is high up in the organization came to Jason's door (he was still housed) with two police officers to find him because as she noted she had not seen him in some time. With her aid, Jason went back into a detox unit at a local hospital and later into a longer-term rehabilitation program. Jason has become very close with her and other leaders of the organization since that time.

The Los Angeles Community Action Network (LACAN) had an extremely different model because it is a grassroots community organization run by poor people themselves (though it does have an executive director and some staff). Most of its staff, including "core" members (defined based on participation over time) are either poor or were once homeless and/or poor. Most have lived in the Skid Row neighborhood. The variance in two advocate/activists of LACAN who were homeless is shown by Tyrone, a sixty-three-year-old African American veteran who walks with a cane, and Rick, a youngish-looking twenty-seven-year-old white man with an eager smile who came to Los Angeles to be a "movie star."

Like many older people I met in Skid Row, Tyrone grew up in a large and religious family. He grew up in Florida and went into the Navy in 1972. There he learned welding skills, which served him for many years to lead an existence that many would consider middle class, with a wife who was a surgical technician. In the 1980s, Tyrone says he and his wife "kind of lost interest in each other," and that, along with stress of a new job (he was hurt in an accident and was retrained to repair photocopiers) led him to drugs. Along with many others at that time, he was a victim of the crack epidemic. Homeless for nearly five years, he came to Skid Row and lived in the various SRO hotels. He was arrested around 2008 for selling drugs to an undercover officer, but he felt that the judge was fair in offering a way out of the sentence if he underwent rehabilitation.

Tyrone speaks of a strong need to "give back" to others who are going through a similar situation. He met LACAN in the course of his living in the SROs, when he had a lot of problems with the management. He says many of the owners are "slumlords," keeping people in "horrible conditions." He gained some experience working with LA-CAN in organizing the residents of one particularly notorious SRO. Tyrone also has experienced the police brutality that is rather legendary in Los Angeles. Police jumped him from behind, put him in a choke-hold, and pepper-sprayed him. He was held for suspicion of having "nunchucks," a word I had not heard for a police tool to control people (Tyrone said that he had not heard it before either). Although Tyrone was never charged, the attack on him reaggravated his spinal injury, causing him severe pain. Tyrone, now active in LACAN for more than five years, is not only a "core" member but has been asked to join the board of directors of the organization.

Rick, twenty-seven, is a much newer member of LACAN and its core than Tyrone. He is from Birmingham, Alabama, where he came from a middle-class family. Always a lover of film, he was a projectionist as a youth. Rick decided some years ago to leave Birmingham and go to Hollywood to seek his fame in the entertainment world. Like many people I interviewed in Los Angeles, not only were his great hopes not met, but a series of events including drug use led to him being out on the streets. He squatted for a long time, but at one point entered the service system, only to be kicked out of a residence for using drugs. Meanwhile as Occupy! was unfolding in 2012, and through a series of contacts on the streets including LACAN, he became involved in the movement and occupation. Unlike other cities where homeless people and protestors were at odds, in Los Angeles a series of meetings helped diversify the protest and make it more representative racially and class-wise of the nearby population. Rick became very impressed with LA-CAN and also made some close friends among the members. He has now been active for a couple of years and gets a stipend for being the lead organizer at LACAN for a campaign to enact a "Homeless Bill of Rights" in the state legislature (this would guarantee homeless people the right to stand, sit, rest, sleep, eat, and perform other daily activities without fear of arrest or harassment). Moreover, in the last year a number of acting gigs have come to him. Rick is a member of the LAPD, the Skid Row–based avant-garde theater, for which he gets a stipend, and moreover has landed a part in a short film out of Hollywood. Enthusiastic, Rick feels optimistic about his theater/film career and is committed to LACAN as well.

In Washington, DC, my focus group with advocates who were all affiliated with the National Coalition for the Homeless (NCH) was very impressive to me. All eight were formerly homeless people; they were all highly articulate spokespeople whom one can imagine being persuasive in their missions to educate the public and even schoolchildren on what homelessness is like and how it could be ended. Somewhat randomly, I will describe two advocates I met: Arnie, a burly, strong fifty-six-year-old African American man who had been a federal law enforcement officer before he was homeless, and Dwayne, a thinner white forty-year-old formerly homeless man who talked with a surprisingly self-effacing humor during the interview.

Arnie, like several of the people interviewed in Washington, DC, said he used to have a "very negative opinion of homeless people. I just assumed they were lazy people. I would never in my whole life have ever thought I would be homeless, I would have bet you anything that I would not." He grew up in a middle-class family, and as a federal law enforcement officer married to a working wife, they made $200,000 a year. "We had the fancy house, a boat, high-class cars, you name it." But a serious case of undiagnosed bipolar disorder changed all that, and in a few years he lost everything. His wife, his job, and his belongings went. He lost a lot of money through gambling and began "self-medicating" for his disorder with alcohol and drugs. He was homeless for six years, three outside of the shelters, and three inside. Arnie hit even worse luck when he was attacked by robbers and sustained three gunshot wounds; he had to have four surgeries. Arnie hit "rock bottom" and was at the point of suicide, but then a case manager got him to go for a psychiatric consultation, and he was placed on medication that eased his bipolar disorder.

Arnie does feel that it is important to "give back" to his fellows as well as telling his moving story. He is not only on the Coalition for the Homeless' Speakers' Bureau, which educates the public and politicians about homelessness, but he has a position now with the Friendship House, a nonprofit organization in Washington, DC. Like the advocates paid a stipend by the organization in Portland, it is not clear to me whether the members can deviate in their speeches or activities of the broader organization. In this sense both they and the Portland advocates are quasi-employees, unlike Theodore who is his own boss.

Dwayne, a forty-year-old white formerly homeless person, has a different background from Arnie. Born in Colorado Springs, Colorado, he describes himself as being from "a family that did not get along." He says he was "a weird kid" who was difficult to get close to. He did work in the restaurant business until he was twenty-nine, but then he lost his job and his housing. He became a wanderer and went to Texas, New Mexico, Arizona, Ohio, St. Louis, Missouri, and New York City, among other places. Because he is somewhat small in frame, he was picked on and attacked. Consequently as a homeless person he stayed by himself. He came to Washington, DC, and after a year and a half there, he was arrested. He felt that this was when "he got lucky" because they had no public defenders, and he had to be given a private attorney. The court let him go; he had to go to a shelter and they set up several conditions, one of which was to have mental health treatment. This was positive for Dwayne because after all those years he discovered what was wrong with him; he was diagnosed as having a schizoid-affective disorder. Moreover, he was required to stay in the shelters. Not all homeless people would consider this a good thing, but in Dwayne's case because he had so isolated himself, he felt this was positive. Like many of the others interviewed in Washington, Dave affirmed that his first contacts with the Coalition for the Homeless gave him some community with other homeless people; for the first time, he recognized that there were many people like him. He got involved in a series of protests with NCH and other organizations over housing and saving shelters and he began serving on their board of directors in 2006. Dwayne is particularly proud of the work he does with school-age children through "the Homeless Challenge" program in which they get to know homeless people. A staff member at NCH praised Dwayne as a "go-to" person to speak to the media and public.

Of course, formerly homeless activists are special people, and do not necessarily exist in every town. Los Angeles and Portland, Maine, for example, have both had movements. But elsewhere in Maine, and in New Hampshire and Haverhill, Massachusetts, they did not. Certainly major cities are likely to have at least some grassroots advocates, particularly those with an active history of protest and activism.

SOME NOTABLE SURVIVAL STORIES

All homeless people who survive on the streets of America can be considered survivors, but those who made it to "the other side" (became housed) certainly should be. Moreover, very few people dealt with only one challenge called "homelessness"; most dealt with disease (physical and mental), accidents, discrimination, abuse, substance issues, and other problems that sometimes made homelessness pale in comparison.

Several people I met faced such an array of problems and issues that in the interview I thought, "how did they make it here?" or "how did they make it as intact as they are?" Although perhaps we could say this about many of the people interviewed, to me the most dramatic were

Mindy, who suffered from neurofibromatosis (commonly referred to as "Elephant Man's disease");

Wally whom we met briefly earlier and who nearly died in an accident and was quadriplegic for years;

Christie, a transgendered woman who had to struggle for years with her family, a cult, and her schools to be who she is;

Tillie, who overcame addiction and a mental disorder to go to Howard University in Washington, DC;

Ronnie, who was leading an average life before sustaining one loss after another in his family and, in addition, was in a fight and sustained an accident that nearly took his life; and

Fiona, an older woman who after her husband died depended on her family, who stole from her, which eventually left her homeless and extremely distraught.

The first three were interviewed in Los Angeles; Tillie in Washington DC; Ronnie in Haverhill, Massachusetts; and Fiona in Portsmouth, New Hampshire.

I can't imagine anyone not feeling sorry for Mindy, a fifty-four-year-old African American woman who lives in Skid Row, Los Angeles. What was amazing to me is that not only does she not feel sorry for herself, but she said proudly that she loves her life. Even before she had neurofibromatosis, Mindy suffered a very hard life: she was raped and abused as a child, and was put into foster care. She began to suffer depression early in her life. She had a total of twelve children with different men. Then she was diagnosed with her disease. Mindy has a combination of pockmarks and growths coming from whatever parts of the body can be seen, but she assured me that it was even worse under her clothes. She has been made fun of and spat on all her life. "I had to get used to the looks on people's faces. Now I really do not care." But it was not just looks as a poor, African American woman with her disability; she is seen as a leper. In one incident she mentioned, she went to shop for some new clothes after she obtained her first disability check from Social Security. She went to a store at the ground floor of a hotel in Los Angeles. She was selecting and trying on clothes when a salesperson came at her with a broom and started striking her. Before she knew it, a police officer arrived and soon had his knee on her back. Evidently to the salesperson and officer, this woman must be a thief; she did not belong in this hotel store. "I was never so humiliated in my life," says Mindy; "I was not arrested or anything, but I was laid low." She says people do not often show kindness. "I was dying of thirst one day from walking and I asked this (very middle-class) lady for water," Mindy remembers, "she brings me back a warm cup of water" on this hot day.

However, this does not describe the worst. Evidently, neurofibromatosis can be a terminal disease and becomes cancerous. She has had cancer twice, including breast cancer. She has had radiation and chemotherapy, and she said, "all the doctors can do is pray it is gone." When I met Mindy, she did not know her latest prognosis, but when I saw her several days later she did tell me happily that her latest tumors were benign.

I have interviewed people with many severe problems, but what was striking about Mindy, despite her homelessness, disease, and history, was how happy she is. She began her interview not with any of this, but talking about her acting career. I knew she was an active member of the LAPD (Los Angeles Poverty Department, the avant-garde stage theater) but she proudly told me of her role in the movie *The Soloist*[7] a number of years before as well as a film about Skid Row called *Lost Angels: Skid Row Is My Home*.[8] She loves acting and was part of a group from the LAPD that visited the Netherlands in 2008.

But even more important to her is that she has "her honey." She met her boyfriend fourteen years ago, and she said it is the first and only time she had experienced unconditional love. They live in the same apartment building on two separate floors. She is a bit worried about her beau now; he is older than she is and has had spinal cord surgery and prostate problems. The two of them go to church together, sing and dance; he comes to her plays, and they go to Skid Row events. The community of Skid Row was as much a part of her feeling of well-being as the other factors. "I live here because of my honey, but also the talent, the innocence, the compassion and the love people down here have," Mindy affirmed. As we will discuss later, the strong aspects of solidarity in the housed Skid Row community was one of the things that most impressed me as well.

Mindy remarked that it has taken her many years to get to this point. She has worked extensively with a therapist and holds strong spiritual beliefs. She firmly notes, "I learned to love myself because no one else did. I just have to keep going and wash away the tears." This kind of testimony, which I was to hear more than I ever expected, makes one wonder what incredibly better coping skills some of the poor and homeless have that perhaps the average middle-class person may not.

Wally, mentioned above, was another example of dreadful circumstances, yet he has a personality very much at ease with himself and very "grateful he found his sanity" on Skid Row. Wally's life seems always full of contradictions; it was harsh, but he had many strengths and achievements. For example, he was taken away from his mother because of abuse, but lived with an uncle, which turned out to be a blessing in disguise; he feels "it was my real family . . . they treated me as a human being." He was his high school's class president and then went to the University of Tennessee for his BA. He went into the military after college and there was assigned to a special combat unit. He tells a harrowing story of being shot on the way out of a mission and almost dying. Still he recovered and got his master's degree from the University of Illinois. He became a teacher of English as a second language. Unfortunately, four years later, his principal criticized him for not having enough "real-life experience" and fired him. Wally became a "beach bum" in a tony Southern California coastal town, where he got to know the son of a neighbor who urged him to join his family's pool business.

It was unfortunately while an inspector for the pool business that Wally had the horrific accident that crushed him from the neck down. He was given no chance of recovering from being a quadriplegic. In the two years he was in a medical hospital, Wally lost all his money, his girlfriend of four years, his car, and all his friends. "They couldn't figure out how to act and then avoided me," recalls Wally, who says even his own brother, who lived nearby, did not visit. It was "the deepest, darkest moment of my life." Distraught, Wally was moved to a veterans' hospital psychiatric ward, where he was on the "Thorazine shuffle." Amazingly, one day he felt a tingle in his legs and it was the beginning of his recovery, which took some years (and he is still on physical therapy). He went on and off the streets, then to another VA hospital and several years later he was finally placed in SRO in Skid Row.

Like Mindy, it is remarkable how resilient Wally is. He said he surprised himself by finding a community in Skid Row. It brought sanity back to him. What really matters became clearer. "When you have nothing, you can only give of yourself. Here we feel a certain safety in numbers. We feel less stigma because we have all been there," Wally remarks. He began being "Mr. Fixit," helping people build walls and fences, and even sweeping streets. He became an activist with LACAN and was an intern there for a while. He is involved in LAPD and the Skid Row Players. Wally, a handsome middle-aged African American, shows no sign of disability or even age (I guessed he was in his thirties when he asked me at first); many formerly homeless look older than they are. Wally is still in court battles over the accident and with the Veterans Administration and the company that built the pools, but like Mindy, he is not an angry person. He is articulate and pleasant, and talks with great passion and knowledge about life in Skid Row.

Christie, a large African American transgendered woman who is enthusiastic and talkative as the current LACAN intern, did not suffer the physical illness or accident that Mindy and Wally did. However, her harsh upbringing, her poverty, and then her questioning of her gender led to huge problems in her life with her family and schools, and eventually helped propel her into homelessness. Studies have shown a very high number of LGBT homeless people particularly among youth;[9] however, only recently has attention been paid to adult homeless people, particularly transgender. After a difficult childhood, she got involved at twenty with the "Dream School," a residential Christian-run school widely viewed as a cult. For nearly eight years, she went back and forth to the school, to homelessness, to some shared housing, to "couch surfing" and back. In retrospect, Christie finds it hard to explain why she kept going back to the Dream School, which made clear their disdain for her and any deviation from their path. The first time they kicked her out was when they found the gay newspaper *The Advocate* in her room. She struggled over those years with her identity, and being not ready to affirm her sexual orientation, she felt that she had to go back as it was her residence. Her family rejected her. Her mother still acts as if she knows nothing of her sexual orientation, but clearly she disapproves. Her nephew suddenly charged her with sexual abuse and the family believed him. She started school at Los Angeles City College and enjoyed it, and is clearly a very bright person. However, as with many people who are homeless, she found it nearly impossible to attend the right classes while also making the deadlines to get across town in Los Angeles to the shelters (shelter hours, often including long lines before they open, are notorious for making work, school, and other obligations impossible). She asked the school for an emergency loan, but they said they did not have such a thing. Her homelessness tended to be episodic, lasting for months at a time, six months at the most. In between she sometimes was back tolerating the Dream School or rooming with a transgendered person she had met but who had a terrible temper. With no source of income, a battle with either one (the school or her roommate) landed Christie on the streets.

While Christie began getting familiar with the homeless services, the real change was finding groups of like-minded people, first a group called "Friends," an LGBT group. She was able to get into a "wet" shelter (one that tolerates drink or drug use or at least does not evict people) called "Rainbow" and she also connected with the Downtown Women's Advocacy Coalition (DWAC). Her coming out as transgendered pretty much paralleled her getting an apartment in Skid Row. She always had a love of theater and now in addition to working with LAPD and LACAN, she also participates in the Theatre of the Oppressed and the Pop-Up Theatre. She says, "at first I was deeply scared of Skid Row, but it is a community, and people get to know you and they protect you." She is certain she wants to finish college; she has a strong thirst for knowledge, and asked me many questions about universities.

Tillie, a fiftyish African American woman whom I met in the focus group in Washington, DC, reminded me again, as did Mindy, Wally, and Christie, how problems can pile up on problems and despite the overwhelming burden, people carry on. Tillie was a child of government workers and described her growing up as a middle-class environment. The loss of her father at an early age "made her look for love in all the wrong places" and she got into drugs. For a long time, Tillie was a "functional addict" able to work during the week and confine her use to the weekends. But in her early forties, she lost her apartment while she was pregnant. She became homeless while in the early stages. She says, "If it wasn't for my fourteen-year-old I would be dead." She credits wanting her baby's life to be different from hers as providing the commitment to get off drugs. She went to detoxification at DC General Hospital and then to the House of Ruth, a group home for ex-addicts, for eighteen months. She also received a diagnosis of bipolar disorder. She began college at the University of DC. Around that time, however, she got involved with a man much younger than she and he became abusive toward her. He was finally arrested, says Tillie, not for anything he did to her, but for stalking another woman. "I never thought I was worth anything," she exclaimed in the interview, "but now I know I am." While struggling with her relationship and housing, she was able to finish a bachelor's degree at Howard University, a very well-regarded university. But, while housed now for a while, she has asthma from living in her house, which is filled with mold, and has become ill; according to the doctor she may have kidney cancer. At that point in the interview she broke into tears, but afterward she regained her composure and passed around a drawing of a room she had designed (she works as an interior designer).

Ronnie, a forty-seven-year-old man I interviewed in Haverhill, Massachusetts, may take the prize (with Mindy) for his Job-like endurance of the many negative events life may offer. Ron grew up in a poor family in central Massachusetts plagued by alcoholism, and he was placed in foster care. But he got along fairly well until about ten years ago. In a five-year period, "I lost everything." First his father died of a heart attack at fifty-eight; less than a year later his mother was dead; and ten months later his brother, only twenty-nine, also died of a heart attack. He kept asking himself what had he done to deserve this. "I was a God-fearing man." His own mental condition began to slip and when he had panic and anxiety attacks and then depression, his wife just could not take it anymore. He worked in construction and began sleeping in his van. He then found a friend he could crash with, but later his friend got a girlfriend and his welcome was gone. He was put on medication, first for depression, and then for bipolar disorder (now he has been diagnosed as having PTSD). But it took a while to find the right medicine and he attempted suicide with an overdose of medications. "God must have wanted me alive!" he exclaimed.

While trying to get back on his feet, but now homeless and using services, waiting for his application for his disability benefits, he had another setback. He no longer remembers exactly what happened, but he almost died. Somehow, someone captured it on tape. A man took a swing at Ronnie and he fell backward and sustained a fractured skull. He demonstrated how the long part of his skull was cut open. He was medevaced to Beth Israel Hospital in Boston. He had already had "brain bleed." He was told he was very lucky to have survived and was in the hospital for ten days. He still has physical therapy, his balance is off, his speech can be odd, and for a long time he could not ride a motorcycle, which he loves.

Ronnie is much better now. He recently moved into a disabled/senior housing complex (he is receiving Social Security disability). His ex-wife and he are now on good terms, and his two children, seventeen and fifteen, visit him regularly. He quotes his therapist, who he said held up her pad and said she was amazed at what he had lived through. She felt that *she* could not take hearing about it anymore.

One of the things that impressed me about Ronnie was his acceptance of his diagnoses and his friendships based on them. Two people I had interviewed nearby in Haverhill, Dora and Dick, were meeting him for dinner. He spoke warmly of these two people, whom he had met while homeless. I knew Dora and Dick also identified as having psychiatric conditions. Like Alcoholics and Narcotics Anonymous, mental health recovery has become a vehicle for community and comradeship as we will discuss further in the book.

Although perhaps not competing with Mindy and Ronnie for the Job-like award, sixty-two-year-old Fiona from Portsmouth, New Hampshire, interrupted her interview with copious tears. First off, to say the least, it is very difficult to first become homeless in the mid-fifties and to be off and on homeless in your sixties. Her early and middle life in no way prepared her for the suffering she underwent. After both her husband and mother had died prematurely, Fiona was evicted from a home she lived in in northern Massachusetts. Unable to pay the rent in that tony area, she went to the only place that had a shelter bed: Crossroads, the homeless agency in Portsmouth. She has been off and on homeless with a daughter in an area not terribly friendly to homeless and poor people. But the subject of most of her tears was her exploitative treatment by her son-in-law and daughter. They had finally found a new apartment while Fiona, like a lot of poor and homeless people, awaited approval of checks from the government. When her largest payment arrived, Fiona was not told about it, but her son-in-law forged her name on a large check and deposited it in his account. She still does not believe that he could do it, not to mention that her own daughter would stand for it and agree with him to evict her when she could not pay the rent. Her son-in-law is now incarcerated at the state prison in Concord, New Hampshire, but she feels she cannot forgive her daughter. "I hate to say it but I want to see her punished too."

Fiona, a religious woman, makes no bones about her fears, although she had just gotten into a senior/disabled housing complex in Portsmouth. She told me, "Forgive me, Jesus, I can't be homeless again. I will kill myself!"—this in spite of the fact that as others have also commented, "the homeless people I have met are the nicest people. They will give you the shirt off their back. They are a lot nicer than the other [citizens]." Still, to live at sixty-two in the cold winters of New Hampshire seems quite horrendous, and Fiona now has been diagnosed with COPD (chronic obstructive pulmonary disease). She had every reason to cry.

Shirley and Sandy

Two other individuals interviewed are of interest because their bouts with homelessness are so representative of many other people's issues. Shirley, a fifty-two-year-old woman living in Los Angeles's Skid Row, suffered repeatedly from domestic violence at the hands of boyfriends and husbands, and Sandy, now fifty-nine, like many other people, was cut off from benefits for a time, leading him into homelessness.

Shirley, whom people in Skid Row call "Boston," is indeed from the Boston area. She grew up in a chaotic home with an alcoholic father and a mother who abused her physically. She was removed to foster care and "bounced all over the place." She left home extremely unstable emotionally, and started using drugs. One struggle throughout her life was getting help; and she only recently was diagnosed as having a bipolar disorder, which opened the door to a medication that has worked, and also to disability income from SSI. Her adult life has been dominated by domestic violence by abusive men. Shirley explains that these were not poor men, either; they had nice cars and gave her fancy jewelry, snowmobiles, etc. One man almost choked her to death. Even after coming to Los Angeles fifteen years ago, her relationships have been brutal. She moved in with a "very nice man" who was completing his degree and whom she had known for six years. One day he took a barbell and smashed her on the head. The police issued a warrant, but to this day they have not found him. She continues to have a fear of men and any deep involvement with them. (Literature notes domestic violence as one of the top causes of women's homelessness.)[10]

The combination of getting into therapy and her involvement with the Downtown Women's Advocacy Center (DWAC) has helped Shirley get off the streets and regain her sanity. She has won "about ten awards" from DWAC for her service to battered women. Still she finds that type of work "overwhelming," and is not sure she would want to do it as a profession. At the time I interviewed her, she was looking for jobs, and when I met her several weeks later, she had a factory job and was still living in DWAC housing (she has been on a waiting list for Section 8 housing since 2003!).

Sandy was the man in his late fifties mentioned earlier in the context of his house in Amesbury, Massachusetts. Sandy illustrates the dramatic effect of the loss of social benefits at any age. Sandy was a contractor for most of his life, but developed severe injuries from an accident. He stopped work in 2002 and got disability payment through SSI. However, his benefits were cut off by the government because of an allegation that he and several other men were still working. Sandy maintains that the man doing the books erred, and indeed eight months after he lost his benefits, they were restored. However, this was not before he "had the worst year in his and his children's lives."

Sandy's sadness centered on the lives of his two young children, fourteen and eleven, and especially his daughter, who was multiply handicapped. The children spent time in foster care and being bussed forty-five minutes away to a town they did not know. The older boy was able to cope, but his daughter came out "thin as a rail" and bald from "tearing her hair out." In part, the difficulty arose from a custody claim of his ex-wife to the children, but he has now been given custody. He is certainly thankful for having a home again and having his children there. Still, he says it is not easy being poor with his two children and the high prices in New England. He receives only $1,100 a month including food stamps for himself and his two children. He does not have enough money to feed them nutritious food, particularly for his growing fourteen-year-old boy. He complains that the "cost of food is ridiculous at the supermarket."

The profiles in this chapter are meant to acquaint the reader with some people who have been homeless and, in recent years, have become ex-homeless. There is no attempt to argue that they are representative of all ex-homeless people, though they include men and women, people of most ethnicities and races, and people who suffered all the major causes of homelessness. All are united by lack of income to afford housing at some point. Some crises came about as a result of benefit cuts (Sandy); of housing gentrification (TRO, Fiona); of medical crises (Fara, Mindy, Wally); of job loss (Bob, Fara, TRO, Violet, Arnie, Wally); of domestic violence (Shirley, Violet, Tillie); of family conflict (Bob, Fara, Debbie, Violet, Shirley, Tyrone, Arnie, Dwayne, Christie, Tillie, Ronnie, Fiona); of substance use (Bob, Debbie, Cass, Ian, Jason, Tyrone, Rick, Tillie); and some of mental health problems (Shirley, Wally, Theodore, Arnie, Dwayne, Mindy, Tillie, Ronnie). There are many issues that are not often discussed in terms of homelessness such as accidents and physical ailments (like Mindy, Wally, Theodore); robbery (like Arnie); being gay or transgender (like Christie); cults (like Christie); and elder abuse (like Fiona). They also are not uniform in terms of their length of time on the streets; although he did not always identify as a "homeless person" Ian was a street drunk for nearly three decades, and Shirley's homelessness stretched over a decade and a half. At the other end, Fara, TRO, and Sandy were short-term homeless at less than a year. Many are in the middle somewhere with the exact years sometimes a little hazy due to on-and-off homelessness. Overall, their stories show the many ways people enter homelessness and some of the ways they exit homelessness. In the next chapter we look at what seems to be the most basic point of commonality for the homeless—lack of housing—and discuss in more detail how people lose their housing and how it can be regained.

These photos were submitted by eight of those interviewed for the book. "Bob" from the Portland area (top left), "Arnie" from the DC area (top right), "Violet" from the LA area (bottom left), and "Ricky" from the LA area (bottom right).

"Christie" from the LA area (top left), "Ian" from the Portland area (top right), "Louella" from the Portland area (bottom left), and "Wally" from the LA area (bottom right).

3

THE FIGHT TO SECURE AND STAY
IN HOUSING

Americans can accept that the hungry need food. They accept that the
ill need medical care. Yet there is a disconnect when it comes to homelessness. That homeless people need homes should be pretty obvious,
yet many Americans still think of homelessness as an alcohol and drug
problem, a mental illness problem or pathology due to laziness and a
host of personal problems. Advocates have now for nearly four decades
stressed the link between the lack of affordable housing and homelessness with mixed results. Fortunately, despite disagreements among experts about details, there is hardly an expert on homelessness who does
not cite the rising cost of housing since the 1970s as a major factor in
homelessness. Whereas once housing was thought to represent one-
quarter of a family's costs, today there are many who spend half their
income on housing. The losers in the competitive musical chairs for an
apartment are the poorest and most vulnerable people.

A major difference between the people profiled in this book and
homeless people in general is that the vast majority of people in the
book did successfully obtain subsidized housing or equivalent low-income housing. Of fifty-one people interviewed, thirty-one people had
subsidies or vouchers (such as Section 8, described later in this chapter)
and another ten had cheap housing in single room occupancy apartments (SROs), a boarding house, a transitional/supportive residence, or
public housing. Only ten subjects lacked this advantage, and they are a
heterogeneous group including a few more middle-class formerly

homeless people like social worker Fara, community activist Cass, and actor "TRO." Others mostly lived with roommates who were friends. Fiona from Portsmouth, New Hampshire, introduced in chapter 2, actually had an agreement from the senior/disabled housing management where she lived to take only 30 percent of her income even though she had no voucher to require it.

This chapter will describe the overall housing crisis in the United States, and the failure of American social welfare policy in the area of housing (what little policy there is, such as public housing and the Section 8 program). I will discuss the typical struggle our subjects carried out to find housing (many years is common). I will also look at how housing is ignored not only by the public as a solution to homelessness but also by many social service and charitable organizations when it comes to assisting the homeless. I will try to suggest some solutions, but the scope of the problem (for a growing number of Americans, all but the richest) is such that minor reforms are insufficient to meet the need.

THE HOUSING CRISIS

No area of people's budgets has gone up as much in the United States since the 1970s as housing, whether owning a home or renting, except for health care. Housing and health care, as well as longtime fuel costs, wreaked havoc on millions of American budgets. It is as if landlords and housing developers woke in the 1970s to the fact that their profits could soar if they put up fancy new housing, and healthcare providers, insurers, and hospitals saw a wonderful opportunity to increase their profits with expensive medicine.

Just about anyone who is over fifty remembers a time when renting a small apartment in the center of the city might cost a few hundred dollars or less and buying a house might cost $20,000 or $30,000. The huge growth of inflation in the 1970s and 1980s, combined with increasing gentrification particularly in the cities, made housing previously centered on the poor or working class a thing of the past, while rehabilitation turned what had been considered dull and dismal apartments into beautiful condos, co-ops, and luxury housing. There are many cities where an extra "0" has been added to the cost of housing. In cities such as New York, Boston, Los Angeles, Washington, DC, San Francisco, Seattle, and Chicago, for example, it is not hard to find an apartment that rented for $200 in 1978 and now rents for well over $2,000. Similarly, some homes for sale moved from $30,000 to $500,000 if not more in this time.

The best way to see the dramatic change in housing is to see what wage levels would be necessary to live in certain cities. A study called "Out of Reach" done in 2014 by the National Low Income Housing Coalition (and using the Department of Housing and Urban Development's own cost estimates) found that nationwide, in order to afford rent on a one-bedroom apartment, someone needs to earn at least $18.92 an hour or about $38,000 in annual salary. However, because housing costs vary hugely across the nation, the following costs for the cities that I studied all were higher; keep in mind also that costs have only continued to increase since 2014:

Washington, DC: $28.85 an hour (over $60,000 a year)
Boston, Massachusetts: $27.96 an hour ($58,156 a year)
Los Angeles, California: $26.88 an hour ($55,910 a year)
Haverhill, Massachusetts (not included, likely between Boston, Massachusetts and Portsmouth, New Hampshire): $20.48 an hour ($42,598 a year)
Portland Maine (likely up considerably in the past three years): $19.46 an hour ($40,477 a year)

Expressed another way, in each of the cities studied the majority of the population cannot afford the current housing stock to rent. And this is an understatement because in each city, small or large, there are far more people working in the city who wish to have housing there but have given up. People live as much as eighty miles from Los Angeles or DC to commute there, and while the commutes are not quite so long, an hour commute to Portland, Maine, Portsmouth, New Hampshire, or Haverhill, Massachusetts, is not at all unusual.

There are two additional ways to demonstrate the devastating effect these high rents have. One is to compare the housing wage in these cities with the minimum wage, which is often as much or more than a homeless person can expect: using the minimum wages in 2014 in each city and taking it to compute the percentage of a housing wage it is, one gets the following:

Portland, Maine: 38.5 percent
Haverhill, Massachusetts: 35.4 percent
Los Angeles, California: 33.4 percent
Boston, Massachusetts: 28.6 percent
Washington, DC: 28.5 percent

So the minimum wage is between two-sevenths and three-sevenths of the money one would need to afford the average rent.

The "Out of Reach" study also publishes the renter median income in each city. In no city does the average renter make enough to afford the city, although in Washington, DC, it comes close:

Washington, DC, renter's mean: $26.52 ($28.85 housing mean)
Boston, Massachusetts renter's mean: $20.99 ($27.96 housing mean)
Los Angeles, California renter's mean: $18.53 ($26.88 housing mean)
Haverhill, Massachusetts renter's mean: $12.84 ($20.48 housing mean)
Portland, Maine renter's mean: $11.40 ($19.46 housing mean)

Therefore, in Portland, the average renter makes only 58 percent of the housing mean, in Haverhill only 62.6 percent, Los Angeles 69 percent, Boston 75 percent, and DC, 92 percent.

The housing crisis is very important because it frames all issues with homelessness. It affects the service system in an unsaid way, and it affects middle-class people in unstated ways. I believe a major reason that service providers do not immediately proceed with getting newly homeless people into housing (as Kelly, fifty-two years old and a former nurse from DC asked, "Why was it so difficult [to house me]?") is that the service providers themselves do not see housing as a citizen's right, and they often cannot afford the housing they want either. Service providers, like many other people, have assumed since the 1980s that there will be a large number of poor who are excluded from the housing market. Despite the rhetoric about "Housing First" in the homeless advocacy community, most organizations still do not discuss housing in their first interviews, nor do consumers necessarily press providers for housing. It is simply understood that being at a low (or no) level of income means no housing—a situation not at all true prior to about thirty-five years ago. Like health care, Americans have gotten used to the idea that housing is beyond many people's reaches, and while they find it regrettable, they simply acquiesce to this new development. Only radicals seem to see housing and health care as "rights," as is the general view in many other nations and as is declared in the Universal Declaration of Human Rights, among other rights declarations. While health care is a right in almost all other nations, housing rights are more mixed, although some nations do have the right to housing ingrained in law.

Moreover, while high housing costs, on the one hand, make people sympathetic to the poor to some extent, it also normalizes the idea that housing is out of reach. I have met people who voice the idea that if they cannot pay their rent on a social worker's or teacher's or janitor's wages, why should someone not working or with low income have their rent covered? Unfortunately, this negative idea is as prevalent in all likelihood as the altruistic and compassionate idea that all deserve housing. We do not have good studies documenting these attitudes, but compassion may not prevail over feelings of jealousy and competition in the United States.

THE DISMAL GOVERNMENT RECORD

As compared with other nations, there is not much history of government social welfare around housing. Even reformers as early as the late nineteenth century seemed to have looked more to the private sector (for example the invention of the "tenement house" as a reform) than the public sector. Of course to be fair, until modern times housing was a relatively smaller piece of working-class and poor people's budgets, with dilapidated and unhealthy housing being the norm for poor and working people. Since poor and working people could not constitute (and still do not) a profitable market, their needs were left to the marketplace, except where desperation drove employers to develop company housing (or even company towns) to house their own workers. Similarly, outdoor relief to the poor (which was town or city aid to paupers before 1935) in a vague general way could sometimes compensate for housing as part of a general tiny benefit for the poor that might include food, medicine, travel, and lodging (this aid was in kind, not cash, and rarely was very great).

As with many other issues, the New Deal established the first federal program for housing, the 1937 Public Housing Act. Although many people today associate "public housing" with slums and crime, the initial drive for public housing as with the Roosevelt era reforms of social security, unemployment insurance, and public works were aimed at blue-collar and other male breadwinners and their "deserving" families, not the most poor. As a wonderful documentary on public housing in Washington, DC, shows,[1] long lines of tie-and-jacket-clad men (overwhelmingly white) stood on long lines to apply for the first public housing sites. It was only later in American history (particularly from the 1950s on) that the stock of public housing was allowed to deteriorate, that eligibility for public housing was cut so severely that many working-class people were excluded, and that overwhelmingly African American and later Latino/Hispanic people became the vast majority of tenants.

Still, as with many social programs, the Public Housing Act was extremely inadequate. Low-cost housing built by the government, such as public works programs, was visualized as part of the temporary response to the Great Depression, and was always viewed as potentially "subversive" by conservatives who feared that it would be some sort of blueprint for socialism. By 1949, when the Public Housing Act came up for renewal in Congress, a full-scale attack was mounted on it not only by conservatives but by leading landlord and developer groups who used the anticommunism of the period to considerably weaken the potential of public housing, which led directly to what would be severe cutbacks.[2] More important to working-class people at the time was of course the GI Bill, which because of its embrace of nearly free mortgage loans for veterans and their families (as well as other policies such as payment for college and other education) helped lubricate the post–World War II prosperity at least for many white families. With its suburban prejudice, the GI Bill paradoxically hurt the urban areas and led to the growth of suburbs and highways and the sprawl associated with them. It was also of little help to the poor and African Americans, whom segregation kept out of the suburbs.

Like other issues of social policy, the brief period of American prosperity of the "Pax Americana" period (1945–1973) marginalized the poor and those people who advocated for more social benefits. By the 1960s, public housing was firmly associated with inner cities and racial minorities, and the riots of the 1960s added an association with violence and crime. Here were "ghettoized" people who somehow had lost their initiative and their American "get up and go" because they were imprisoned in large, government-run, squalid high-rises. Although for different reasons, many on the left and in the Black Nationalist camp embraced the anti-public-housing rhetoric as much as those on the right. By then the fate of public housing was sealed; its condition in many places would become worse and worse, and because of the very tight eligibility criteria there were relatively few working families who were eligible. The "projects" became filled more and more with the unemployed and welfare recipients.

The growing bipartisan "consensus" against public housing that started back in the 1960s grew into a political agenda by the 1980s and 1990s. The Reagan administration made massive cuts in all areas of HUD (the Department of Housing and Urban Development that had been made a cabinet department in the 1960s). But, as with welfare, it was actually the Clinton administration that put the final nails in the coffin.[3] A bipartisan commission supported a policy in 1992 that has led to gradual preference for privatization of public housing, and according to the Goetz count, has led to a net loss of about 250,000 units of public housing. This loss (about one-fifth of the national units) has occurred at the very time that homelessness has continued to soar, and studies support the conclusion that it is indeed one of the factors in the housing crisis.

Even if the condition of public housing was not so problematic, the fact is that 1.2 million households were in public housing at its height, accounting for perhaps four million people. The poor have been hit with a large decline in the numbers due to both privatization and also the increasingly stricter rules for living in public housing, including immediate eviction of those who have a family member who has had drug charges filed against them. Something as trivial as a marijuana citation can lead to the eviction of not only the charged person, but their whole family. Clearly public housing, with its small number of units, isolated in stigmatized areas, continually underfunded and poorly maintained, is not a solution to anything, but rather is part of America's housing crisis.

SECTION 8: THE "MAJOR" HOUSING AID

A very limited addition to public housing came in 1974 with Section 8 of the Housing and Community Development Act. Not well noticed at the time, the act was one of a large number of "Great Society" type additions made in the Nixon era by a Democratic Congress and an administration not at all opposed to social welfare (for example, the proposal for a guaranteed annual income, the indexing of Social Security to the cost of living, the passage of SSI, and the expansion of the Food Stamp program). Rather than government housing, "Section 8" primarily provides vouchers to eligible tenants to use with private landlords that limit their rents to 30 percent of their income. Because it entailed no expansion of government housing stock and was completely voluntary for landlords (today still no landlord must accept government vouchers) the program was not particularly controversial at the time.

As with all government means-tested programs (eligibility is not an "entitlement" but subject to being at poverty level and acceptance is only tied to the existence of available vouchers) there is a huge gap between the inadequacy and problems of the program and the desperate need of people for the voucher, since it is now (with public housing being cut) really the only government assistance out there (although there are parallel funds from other programs based on it such as Base Realignment and Closure [BRAC] and Housing Plus from the McKinney Act of 1987). As bad as it is, throughout the nation millions of poor people count on some positive surge in the number of Section 8 vouchers, and those who were interviewed sometimes marked the occasion of getting a voucher as would a college student getting into an Ivy League school.

First, because eligibility is set low and its acceptance is entirely voluntary, Section 8 has, like some other welfare programs, become most associated with African Americans and those on welfare. All told, two out of three vouchers go to minorities, and as a recent *New York Times* article showed,[4] minority applicants are essentially funneled into low-income and minority areas within a town or county, whether they wish to be or not. Second, as one of my subjects pointed out, the voucher is essentially a subsidy for the landlords. Lou, a fifty-four-year-old former homeless man from Haverhill, Massachusetts, noted immediately when we talked that he was leaving his housing project in part because his landlord had just announced his second rent increase in a year. Since the government still provides a percentage subsidy, at least a part of the landlord's raise comes from the federal government. Lou thought this was an incredible subsidy to corporate greed; he had found a place with an individual landlord, and said he preferred to live in and negotiate with a non-corporate entity.

Third, since the program has been in constant state of cuts—some emanating from federal administrations, some from Congress, some from the recent state of the sequestration crisis—new vouchers have been frozen quite often in different parts of the nation. Even a rumor of new vouchers produces lines with large numbers of people (in Portland, Maine, a city of only 60,000, it is estimated that 700 people stood in line early in the morning for their first opportunity for vouchers in three years).[5] Many cities have waiting lists reaching eight or ten years, which is quite a devastating blow not only to homeless people, but to others who wish to live in safer or more affordable housing. For example, a woman and children fleeing a building with rats and bedbugs, and another family fleeing violence will share thin hopes for the long queue with homeless people. Moreover, because the release of vouchers tends to start as "word of mouth," and some agencies and organizations receive vouchers, a real possibility of favoritism is introduced into the system. Many of the subjects I interviewed, particularly in the eastern cities of Portland and Haverhill, were extremely happy to receive a voucher, but they were clear that they would not have known a voucher was available but for their caseworker or another worker at a social service agency. As I will discuss below, subjects almost described these vouchers as personal favors. Theodore in Portland ascribed his achieving a place in a senior/disabled housing project as resulting from the work of Catholic Charities, Maine, where he had been a client for many years. He named several workers and therapists, and suggested that a process of planning for this had occurred, including a change in psychiatric diagnosis, which better qualified him. My concern is not so much whether this happened; I wondered whether one had to have struck up not only a client relationship, but become what Michael Lipsky referred to as a "favored client" in order to get help.[6] One professional in Los Angeles said she did not believe the system was engaged in favoritism intentionally, but that favoritism resulted because of the very "catch as catch can" nature of the benefit. Not every organization (much less poor person) is notified that there are vouchers, and so agencies "hustle" to make sure some of the poor people they know who are particularly deserving in their view receive vouchers. (There are two types of vouchers, Section 8 Housing Choice vouchers, which go to the client to find his or her housing, and Project-Based assistance in which aid, usually also 30 percent of housing costs, adheres to the project, not the person.) Perhaps here word of mouth is even more dominant; often the only way of getting into established housing such as senior housing is when someone has died or otherwise vacated the building. Everyone I spoke with agrees that the system of allocation of housing resources, as well as the low number of vouchers available, makes the voucher system problematic.

The greatest problem given the presence of millions of homeless people and the lack of adequate, safe, and affordable housing for millions of others is the inadequacy of vouchers. This is not a new problem traceable to recent administrations or budget deadlocks. In the 1990 edition of his book *Programs in Aid of the Poor*, expert Sar A. Levitan noted

> Since the late 1970s, however, newly subsidized low-income housing units have become increasingly scarce. This shortage is a result of increased demand for low-income housing brought about by increasing numbers of poor families with declining incomes and cutbacks in governmental housing assistance to the poor . . . assistance by HUD to add new units of stock of low-income housing has declined from about $32 billion in 1978 to $10 billion in 1989. . . . In the 1980s [subsidized housing] grew to exceed public housing; various components of Section 8 programs now serve about 2.3 million families. At the same time, however, the federal government has substantially reduced its commitment to supporting construction of lower-income housing.[7]

The strange economics of Section 8 and HUD were already established. As rents rose, a greater proportion of HUD's budget went not to support new subsidies but to finance the ones they already had (due to the fact that landlords simply raise rents). Second, low-income units are being lost to the market since they are subject to deterioration as well as landlord decision that they are unprofitable. Harvard University's Joint Center for Housing Studies (JCH) estimated that 5.6 percent of all low-income housing units were lost between 2001 and 2011. Since the United States has essentially gotten out of the market of building housing, fewer and fewer units exist for low-income people because the market will not provide them.[8]

The JCH report provides the macro-level context of low-income housing. "In 2011 11.8 million renters with extremely low incomes (under $15,000 a year) competed for just 6.9 million rentals affordable to that income cutoff, a shortfall of 4.9 million units. The supply gap worsened after this." Assessing the failure of subsidies, JCH noted that "between the onset of the Great Recession in 2007 and latest count in 2011, the number of such renters [extremely low-income] soared by 3.3 million while the number able to obtain housing assistance expanded by just 225,000. As a result the share of income-eligible households receiving assistance shrank from an already modest 27.4 percent to 23.8%. . . . those with worst case needs (paying more than half their income for housing) jumped by 2.6 million to 8.5 million."[9]

Behind these cold facts and figures lie doubled-up families, homeless families and individuals, and millions of people living in unsafe and unsanitary settings. Note the calculation of 23.8 percent of people helped includes *all* governmental assistance from public housing. In addition, it is based only on the current means test. A graph in the same report (p. 19) probably is more accurate in noting that only 14 percent of rental units are assisted by government funds. This means for the entire rental market of tens of millions of people the nation is providing very little aid.

EXPERIENCES WITH THE HOUSING PROBLEM

To put it succinctly very few, if any, subjects had an easy time getting housing. Few subjects got the "lay of the land" from professionals or other service workers about the programs (or lack thereof) in their community. The assumption that housing was just unavailable or that the rare exception would go to a senior homeless person in an agency or service system is rampant. If you are eating in a soup kitchen or staying in a shelter and are neither asked about permanent housing nor seeing your buddies receive housing, you are not to be blamed for making the assumption that housing aid is not to be had.

The existence of an informal pecking order develops when so many people need housing. Most subjects spent time even when housed in a kind of lower order of housing. For example, in Los Angeles, an SRO hotel room is easier to access but extremely small, sometimes lacking in any kitchen facilities, and in some cases run by absentee landlords who are noted as being harsh. In Portland, because Maine still has a general assistance program (many states have abolished theirs), usually a subject would be most likely to gain his or her first apartment through this program, but aid is provided through a city housing voucher accepted by only a small number of landlords who in turn are not always noted for their quality. This is not to say that there is a conspiracy, but only that the better housing, for example, projects for seniors and disabled or more recent apartments that have some mix of incomes is far harder to find and often these buildings do not have a relationship with social agencies or with city officials who run the general assistance program.

Still another issue is that for many years, workers in the service system assumed that many clients were simply unable to go into housing. Viewing the person in front of them—often a shabby-looking person who was not always well spoken—rather than seeing his or her potentials, many workers concluded that people with substance use or mental health problems (or sometimes just long-term homelessness later described as "chronic homelessness") could not manage "regular" apartments so at best needed to be placed in "transitional" and/or "supportive" housing. Although there is much literature on these programs, in service parlance they are often used interchangeably and refer to group quarters usually run by nonprofit organizations that limit time stays and are "supportive" in the sense of providing services to former homeless people ranging from substance abuse counselors to on-site case managers.

Few people would dispute that certain types of clients do benefit from these programs, and many placed in them like it. But the number of slots is simply too small to rely on them, and many workers exaggerate the benefits of them, and minimize or fail to mention that the person will once again be out on the pavement looking for another apartment in a certain amount of time. Nonprofit organizations have their own self-interests as well in promoting housing they themselves run. In many cases, these places have deteriorated to quasi-shelters (or resemble the poorhouses of old) because they lack adequate staff, take in too many people, or have insufficient services.

Even today when "Housing First" is the motto of some advocates, a serious commitment to this is absent. For example, in Portland, Maine, city officials and many providers make much of a new document that clients must sign at the shelters, which, among other things, commits them to meet with workers and plan for housing. Yet the housing market is not in client hands, and there is no obligation for the city or social service providers to give more than a list of landlords to clients. It is a case of "old wine in new jugs"; the city is maintaining its right to eventually show some homeless people the literal (shelter) door if they do not "work" on themselves, including whatever problems are identified. But there is no equal commitment by anyone to provide housing. Historically what usually happens is that in addition to some homeless people being eventually thrown out of a shelter, a larger number remain in the system while going unhoused because no one has a good idea where their housing will come from. Much rhetoric is thrown out, but few resources follow.

Kelly's declaration that she spent seven years without housing and being told there was none, and then suddenly getting housing is not at all unusual, although of course many homeless are not homeless that long. This may seem amazing, but the fact is that the social service system does not promote housing as a commodity the way food or clothes are provided. If a client says he needs one of these former resources, they will likely be immediately sent to a soup kitchen or clothes closet. But a request for housing is not met in a coherent way in my experience. At best, an agency will have a list of landlords who rent to low-income people. A homeless person I met and worked with had such a document, which contained many phone numbers that were out of order or continuously busy. This is the same list the city provides to clients at general assistance. Therefore, housing becomes a sort of game in which people go through the process but with insufficient aid to get the kind of housing they need, much less support for whatever special requirements they have. To be fair to all, social service providers and landlords do not have a magic stock of housing either. The system is stuck in its past practice. For example, a landlord not approved for general assistance payments (there are only a few) cannot simply say "OK put a homeless person here" unless of course they do so without any assurance of payment. When agencies get vouchers for housing, obviously they do suddenly move from the slow pace to a more rapid one once there are more vouchers available.

TWO ENDS OF THE SPECTRUM

Perhaps a more nuanced view comes from thinking about subjects' interviews in two different parts; some formerly homeless people, especially in Haverhill and to a lesser extent Portland, tended generally to praise their social workers/case managers and express satisfaction, if not with the entire experience of trying to be rehoused, at least with the final step in their rehousing. This attitude was almost totally absent in the larger cities of Los Angeles and Washington, DC. I do not think, given our relatively small sample, that there is any scientific way to explain this difference; it may be more a function of certain homeless people (particularly in Haverhill) having a short-term experience with homelessness as opposed to others who were homeless for many years. Or it may be a factor of the smallness of these two cities as opposed to greater impersonality in large cities. There is also a major racial difference in the parts of the sample with the smaller cities being predominantly white. Some combination of these factors made subjects in the two northeastern cities more personally appreciative of the service system and of the rehousing efforts as opposed to subjects in the other cities.

More importantly, the examples provide us with more experience in examining the pathways out of homelessness, what seems to work better and what does not, and perhaps some hunches as to why. Without regard to the specific cities, they do tell us something about the homeless and housing experience.

The great happiness and satisfaction of several of the former homeless people in Haverhill—for example Sandy, Dora and Dick, and Ronnie—illustrate the appreciation of some short-term homeless people. As mentioned in chapter 2, Sandy was the fifty-nine-year-old with two young children who was homeless for less than a year after being cut off from disability benefits. He certainly had some hard times in this period and he expressed plenty of anger at social security, the school, the child protective system, and others. However, he expressed great appreciation for the local service provider, Emmaus Inc. He still brings flowers to a worker who helped him there. As noted, he believes that a lottery held there for a number of subsidized housing units (we do not know whether this was Section 8 or an equivalent) was possibly "fixed" in his favor because of his sympathetic cause (particularly the two kids, one with special needs). Dora and Dick were a middle-aged couple who were also homeless for less than a year through a combination of stress and their preexisting psychiatric conditions. Both expressed considerable criticism about the nature of the shelters in Massachusetts and New Hampshire where they stayed when homeless. Some of the "ridiculous" nature of the "system" was revealed to Dick by how long it took him to receive any benefits because he did not have a Massachusetts identification (they had lived in New Hampshire when they became homeless). While Emmaus worked on the identification issue, they continued to be homeless. Nevertheless, like Sandy, they had high marks for Emmaus, and how they handled their case as well as others. Their situation was a bit different from many I had seen because they appeared to have a single unit of housing in the middle of the city, but it was administratively under the aegis of Emmaus Inc., probably as a form of transitional or supportive housing. Dick said, "We did a dance the day we found out we had housing!" Unlike others they did not seem to have any problems with some restrictions on their actions; no smoking, no drug or alcohol use, and no visitors. These limits seem to have (at least so far) been dwarfed by the fact that it was a "very nice" two-bedroom with some furniture provided by the organization as well as a housing subsidy and a very low capped utility bill.

Dora and Dick expressed what some other poor have internalized; the age-old distinction between those who are "deserving poor" and those who are not. Dick remarked, "You can do OK [at agencies]—there are a lot of heroin and other addicts and they [the agencies] do not like them." But if you are not one of these people, Dick said you have a chance to shine in contrast. While, of course, the remarks are perfectly rational, they do give us one clue as to how some people may be written off as "undeserving" of assistance not only for drugs, but for alcohol, mental illness, misbehavior, crime, or other things that rub the agencies the wrong way.

Of course, where one is placed may also have a great deal to do with satisfaction. Both Ronnie, the forty-six-year-old Haverhill man whose spell of homelessness came about from successive deaths in his family and other losses, and Theodore in Portland were very happy to be in an apartment unit for aged and disabled people. First, these placements, compared to many other options, arguably even "regular" low-income apartments in the community, have a sort of permanency to them that is rare. The services in these complexes are far more than public housing or most Section 8–financed low-income housing provide. At least in the units I visited (including Ronnie and Theodore as well as Charley, a fifty-nine-year-old former homeless man who lived in the same building as Theodore) there were good new elevators and disabled access, clean floors and common areas with many posters of upcoming events, and a host of maintenance people at work. Because of their association with seniors, the buildings have low stigma. Theodore is one of the most scathing critics of the "system." He was glad that a combination of his issues and help from his social workers allowed him to move into senior housing, but it can be a bit isolated from the centers of the city he has frequented and from social services. The fact that he met his fiancée in the building has made a great difference.

Bob, Ian, Jason, and Louella of Portland are also examples of relatively satisfied formerly homeless clients. For both Bob and Ian, the men in late middle age profiled in chapter 2, the viewpoint of recovering alcoholic framed much of their comments. As is typical of strong proponents of recovery, they were usually far more critical of their own actions than others were. But both also had a relatively straightforward time in gaining housing. Bob was housed for two years in a group home for substance users as rehabilitation, and through the aid of a therapist he obtained a subsidy that provided him security in a fairly nice room in a roomy house. Ian, who spent the better part of his life as an alcoholic, credits a steady friend with getting him to Portland and recovery. He was homeless for three years, but finally got disability benefits and a housing subsidy through an agency in the city. Ian is extremely grateful to everyone who aided him. Jason, as noted in chapter 2, has close ties to a service organization, and he has only positive words for the workers there who help him get rehoused when a relapse with alcohol caused another round of homelessness. Louella, a twenty-nine-year-old former homeless woman living in Westbrook, Maine, near Portland, was impressed that workers in Portland even mentioned housing, recalling that the help she received in Massachusetts and in the South had never included inquiries about housing. At the time, Portland still had some housing vouchers for the homeless and were targeting "chronic homeless," a term she had neither heard of nor identified with, but for which she qualified.

In sum, under certain circumstances, particularly in these smaller cities, and with the availability of housing vouchers targeted at "good" candidates, rehousing people can be achieved. As with all successfully rehoused homeless people, they were in the right place at the right time.

Subjects in the larger cities by no means trashed the service system or focused criticism on social agencies. They simply did not mention them, attributing their success either to their own actions or to assistance from advocacy or political groups or their ability to fight for what is right. Although as a general rule some might say they were more political in outlook, several formerly homeless people above, particularly Theodore and Jason, were also political activists.

Bennie, a thirty-three-year-old man who was homeless in Portsmouth, New Hampshire, made many criticisms of the city and its service system. Now in a boarding house, he was unhappy with this situation, and spoke of the other residents as being almost "all alcoholics." Most interesting was his commentary on the age of most social workers and other counselors.

"Here is a woman maybe twenty-five and she makes decisions over your life, like when you are being thrown out of the shelter. I mean what experience does she have? [The] last one told me how she owes so much money on her [credit] card, she does not know what to do. How can she counsel other people when she does not know?"

Many African American formerly homeless people had deep criticisms of their experiences even when they personally had pulled through. Lou, as we have seen in Haverhill, was critical of his landlord and the way Section 8 and other subsidies were used to make them rich. Mary and Sally, middle-aged African American women from Los Angeles, and Tillie, a middle-aged African American woman in Washington, DC, were all involved with lawsuits with their landlords. They were all firm that they would not stand for unhealthy conditions for their children and families that were the fault of the landlord. Of course, some of these formerly homeless people were at different stages of their ex-homelessness. Tillie, for example, has been housed for several

years and obtained her BA at Howard. She is suing her landlord about
mold and the development of asthma from it. She has Section 8, but
noted that the landlord was trying to cut down on his Section 8 apartments. Such an ironic twist is not at all unusual; landlords sometimes
find a different marketing strategy helps them make more money. Sally,
a middle-aged African American in Los Angeles, also believes gentrification is behind her landlord's strategy to get her and others out ("they
thought I was ill and would not fight it") and replace the current tenants
with Korean Americans (she lives near Koreatown in Los Angeles).

But it was not just "political" people or African Americans who had a
critical attitude toward the housing system. My students at CSUDH
profiled earlier, Debbie and Violet (chapter 2), as well as Martha, fifty-
one, all of whom themselves want to be counselors of some sort, did not
mention the service system or credit a worker. They were certainly not
ungrateful for achieving a voucher because all three had children and
were desperate for housing. But again, perhaps in part because of their
long experience as housed people, they tended to credit themselves
with what achievements they made. Violet discusses her ability to avoid
arrest or harassment while living out of a vehicle in Long Beach. She
was able to maintain jobs and become a paralegal while going to school.
She is the only one I interviewed who now owns her home. Debbie,
with the aid of her grown children, was able to stay in her apartment
when it was no longer a "Section 8" apartment. Martha has had many
experiences all her life with public and subsidized housing and credits
her mother's close friend with getting her on "an apartment list" for
housing.

Several things are apparent here. One is that those who experience
more limited time as homeless and are lucky enough to get aid relatively quickly are likely to be more appreciative than others. Those who are
more veterans of homelessness and also of the service system are generally more critical. Years of experience shows them that even adequate
subsidized apartments are subject to being changed to non-subsidized
housing and to the forces of gentrification that are spreading so rapidly
into new areas (this was most apparent in Los Angeles). While many
factors of personality or political views of individuals can be considered,
perhaps most notable is the harsh experience of being pushed out again
after being rehoused. There really have not been enough studies longitudinally of low-income people and the long-term effects of being

pushed in and out of the low-income market, public housing, and subsidized housing, not the mention other forms of housing such as transitional housing, boarding homes, or SROs.

THE DIFFICULTY IN HOUSING SOLUTIONS

Although many would agree with the idea that housing is every bit as important as other basic needs such as health care or food, there is very little consensus even among reformers as to what to do about housing. Although housing in the United States certainly mirrors the commodification of health care in its thousands of centers of profit throughout the country, the knowledge that health care has been greatly decommodified in many nations provides a degree of hope among American reformers and certainly radicals (e.g., the possibility of universal single-payer health care remains alive even after the continued fragmented efforts at reform). At least to my knowledge, there is no experiment with abolition of profit from housing on a grand scale. At best, we can point to many social democratic nations that have a much larger sector of publicly supported housing that, while it cannot compete with the private sector in luxury or space, can at least secure more affordable homes to the general population. Many European nations provide a larger sector of public or social housing (sometimes administered through nonprofit groups) than the United States.

The proposal that the government build a large number of apartment buildings throughout the country, while clearly not in the offing as far as can be seen, seems a most pragmatic measure. This would not only provide more housing in an extremely tight market, but flooding the market has some chance of restoring more affordable housing. The idea, similar to the 1930s idea of public housing, is often paired with providing employment to the jobless in a strategic move to assist both workers and low-income or working-class people as consumers. No doubt the failure of even general proposals to succeed so far can be attributed to a number of likely opponents. Landlord and developer groups, as well as much of the associated industry, would oppose such proposals for fear of losing money. The issue of where to put housing (the "not in my backyard" phenomenon) becomes prominent when planners get around to being specific as to where more housing would go. Even advocates seem to face a dilemma of having more housing, but segregated by class and race, because more powerful opponents will make sure that "their" neighborhoods are not "invaded" by public housing.

Yet despite these forces, it seems the basic divide will remain—more housing for the poor or those near poverty is supported by advocates and some groups such as unions. Middle- and upper-class groups will be opposed. Other reforms are shot down even more quickly. Many cities in the United States embraced rent control in the Second World War and while many have abolished it, some still have remnants. Unfortunately, attempts to strengthen rent control have usually failed, and even popular support can be weak in the face of landlord (and media) opposition arguing that the market for housing will dry up if too many price controls are put in place.

If prices cannot be controlled, certain types of housing subsidies will be another method to help control costs, at least for some groups of people. Still, it is not as if the housing subsidies through Section 8, for example, are at all popular; they face the constant popular stigma about low-income people associated with all "welfare" programs. There are partial exceptions such as senior citizen housing and now veterans' subsidies, but for the most part it is hard at this moment to see great support for more subsidies for decent apartments that are not racially and class segregated.

Therefore, unfortunately, unless we enter a very different political era, at least akin to the 1930s or the 1960s–1970s, it is hard to imagine massive housing reform. Unlike health care, fewer middle-income and upper-income people come into contact with absolute housing need. That is, well-publicized stories of even some affluent people losing insurance has provided some universality to the demands for change in health care. But even though grumbling may be heard, most middle-class people are buffeted from the worst in the housing system, unless they experience tremendous downward mobility, which then means they are no longer middle class. The next chapter turns from housing to income, which may provide upward or downward mobility.

4

THE INCOME TO LIVE AND AVOID HOMELESSNESS

Whatever the blame that homelessness and issues such as mental health or substance use give rise to, being housed requires first, access to affordable housing, and, as I shall discuss here, the income to pay for it as well as necessities such as food, transportation, utilities (sometimes, although now less often, covered by rent), clothing, and at least a minimum amount of money to spend on entertaining oneself. All else is quite secondary if you do not have these resources.

Once again, subjects had moved out of homelessness by, among other things, gaining a secure source of income. They are, of course, hardly alone, but rather are among millions who do so. This point needs stressing because while we do not wish to forget for a moment the other hundreds of thousands to millions who lack even these resources and are homeless, it is a significant point. For most of the people interviewed, despite the public's call to "get a job," the income mostly came from social benefits rather than full-time jobs, although it was often combined with *some* work income, rather than being able to live on full-time earnings. Fully forty-three of the fifty-one subjects had either a social benefit that came close to meeting their needs[1] or a full-time equivalent job. Benefits far outweighed the jobs, with twenty-five subjects having either retirement, Social Security disability, or veterans' pensions; nine had SSI (Supplemental Security Income, explained in more detail later in the chapter); and nine were working either full-time or its financial equivalent. Only eight subjects lacked a full-time job or a significant social benefit source.

This chapter will begin with an overall discussion of the lack of adequate jobs, particularly well-paying jobs, in America, and the lack of social benefits available to most Americans in replacing income due to unemployment, retirement, disability, child care, or other important reasons. We will then examine the study findings, and explore further how the subjects were able to use available resources to support themselves.

THE MYTH OF "GETTING A JOB"

Over the many years since homelessness returned to the United States, I have often heard the comment of angry citizens saying, "Go get a job!" directed at homeless and other poor people (usually it is difficult for citizens to tell who is homeless or not, much less who is working or not) as if this simple idea never occurred to the people they are admonishing. Obviously, it is a lay critique of the poor person's situation as stemming from his or her lack of motivation. Such statements are ludicrous on several fronts: they ignore the fact that many homeless people *do* work, but do not have enough income from their jobs to live in even the cheapest of housing; they ignore the strong discrimination among employers against homeless people and other poor people who do not look "appropriate"; and finally, they fail to acknowledge that all classes except the rich have experienced a job crisis, with wages not going up for most workers in this nation in real terms since 1973, as well as a real decline in jobs that once held greater satisfaction, from craftspeople to some professional jobs.

The number (or percentage) of homeless people who are working is difficult to calculate because of the fluidity of life on the streets (and low-income work) as well as the uncertainty of what is being counted for "work." In an article in *Social Work*,[2] I noted that many poor people work in the "underground economy" of unregulated labor, or as Snow and Anderson have called it, "shadow work."[3] These may be illegal (drug sales, prostitution) but are more often just casual labor (day labor, gardening or yardwork, ad hoc work on the docks, etc.) or on the fringe (stripping copper and metals, collecting and returning recyclable bottles, etc.). Some estimates count only work in the official economy, while others count all work. This may lead to an assortment of different figures such as 20 percent, 25 percent, 33.3 percent, or other percentages of the homeless working; it is unknown when in fact the government's labor statistics do not systematically gather such data. As Herbert Gans remarked some years ago, the poor (and now the homeless) serve an important function to capitalist economies by doing the low-paid scut work that other citizens would not, and by being available at short notice in many cities.[4]

Our subjects displayed the diversity of what work consists of. Nine subjects were either full-time workers, or in a case of two actors I judged to be earning close to a full-time salary when interviewed. Five of the nine had degrees: Fara and Cass with their social service backgrounds, Martha, a rehabilitation counselor with her bachelor's degree, Violet a paralegal with a bachelor's degree, and TRO, an actor with an MFA. Rick, who had recently received a film part and worked at LAPD along with TRO, made close to a full-time salary. Miguel (thirty years old now and living in Lewiston, Maine) worked at Dunkin Donuts, and Amelia (a fifty-nine-year-old from Los Angeles) and Shirley both had fill-in factory jobs that approximated close to full-time work. These last three positions were probably more common to homeless and ex-homeless people in the nation than are the first six, although long-term ex-homeless people like Violet, Martha, and Cass are not frequently studied.

However, twenty-four of the remainder had some paid work, making a total of thirty-three people with at least some work. The range again was great. Many people earned stipends from social service or advocacy organizations for the homeless or other service groups. Johnny, a Washington, DC, man who had earlier worked as an electronic technician including for the space shuttle, has a part-time job in electronic engineering again now that he is housed. Laurie, from Los Angeles, did bookkeeping, doing particularly well during tax season. Mary combined doing massage with teaching Japanese massage and writing. But many either had only occasional or sporadic income—Ian selling his paintings or doing paid murals occasionally; Reggie, a forty-eight-year-old former homeless man from LA, played drums in a band and sold nutritional supplements; Jessie, a forty-eight-year-old man, and also Johnny, fifty-seven, both from Washington, DC, made money from selling the home-

less newspaper *Street Sense*, which they had learned could be successful enough to make some money but not enough for a full week's pay. It
was not possible to gain complete accounts of total money earned, but it
would appear that aside from about a dozen of the subjects, most earnings were supplemental to social benefits.

The limits of employment in serving as a barrier to poverty and
homelessness are clear in the biographies of the subjects. For example,
Tyrone was a skilled welder who enjoyed a high standard of living
working on ships. He had an accident in the 1980s, falling from scaf-
folding. His company did have him retrained, and he ended up in a job
repairing photocopiers. Tyrone found the job very stressful as he com-
muted in the Los Angeles area's traffic and covered four counties for
the company. He reinjured himself and received workers' compensation. At that time he and his wife separated. Distraught and without a
work role, Tyrone got into crack cocaine and became homeless. As we
have mentioned above, Johnny, of Washington, DC, had a far more
lucrative position as an electronic engineer with the space program.
Over a period of some years, his mental health problems led to leaving
his family and to his job performance declining. While he deserves a
huge amount of credit for reestablishing himself part-time as an engineer, his losses from poverty and homelessness still cost him much,
including the loss of his security clearance, which he says is critical in
his field.

But job loss can be less dramatic than a fall from high status. Sarah, a
sixty-year-old former homeless woman from Portland, worked many
jobs and at one point worked two jobs, as a personal care attendant for a
family in one of the most affluent towns in the state, while at the same
time working at the popular L. L. Bean store. However, when she lost
her housing, she had to juggle these jobs, transportation to them from
Portland, and the fact that she was sleeping at a transitional residence.
The noise and brightness of the surroundings at the quasi-shelter made
it difficult for her to sleep. Finally, she had to quit one job not only
because of her lack of sleep but because her schedule clashed with the
hours of the residence (this is a very common story for homeless people).[5] Jeremiah, now sixty-six years old, started out in Los Angeles as a
service worker at an agency for the homeless. He, along with several
other workers, found the agency's use of welfare recipients from the
city to do the caretaking work with the homeless, while avoiding mini-

mum wages and benefits, to be abhorrent. Jeremiah with several others took on the agency with the Consumers Affairs Division, the Labor Relations Board, and the Equal Employment Commission, and also tried to unionize. Although many years later the plaintiffs won the case, Jeremiah was blackballed by many of the charitable agencies in Skid Row and found himself without a job or services. The lower-wage social service industry takes its place among the other parts of the low-wage economy.

Therefore, while the point that the ex-homeless (and homeless) *do* work is an important one, it should not be used to obscure the fact that with the current job market in the United States, few good jobs will be available not only to the highly educated, but to those who do not fit very precisely into areas needed by the economy, as more and more college graduates are discovering. If people with BAs can't get other than unskilled jobs, how does that bode for those at the bottom of society? Further, as the examples of Tyrone, Jason, Sarah, and Jeremiah show, "getting a job" is only an answer if you manage to get housing, stay in the job, and avoid getting injured, having a serious breakdown, and ruffling the feathers of the employers you do have.

Because employers have control of the tight labor market, they can refuse labor to anyone with the slightest lack of qualifications, and/or with the slightest deviation in their perceived reliability for work, such as not having an address or a phone, coming in late, wearing shoddy clothes, or smelling. While obtaining housing certainly helps make the person more presentable to the job market, physical remnants of poverty[6] such as being overweight, missing teeth, being in training, or having gaps in a resume make good employment offers rare. Johnny, an example of a highly placed worker who lost his security clearance, illustrates that an episode of difficulty is not resolved quickly because the lack stymied his efforts at a high-level engineering job in the Washington, DC, area. Lack of suitable attire, tools, work socialization, and other problems are likely to continue among those who have experienced poverty.

But added to every low-income person's list of difficulties is also the lack of incentive the job market often presents when one is on governmental social benefits. Those people who receive medical coverage particularly (usually from Medicaid) risk losing it with employment. Many subjects on disability benefits, despite some recent loosening in the rules, fear losing those checks if they work too much. Food stamps and housing assistance are other benefits that, because they are means-tested (i.e., subject to maintaining a certain very low level of income and assets), are subject to being cut off if one makes too much money. It is impossible to capture without speaking to people the great anxiety present in the low-income communities about loss of these benefits. No matter how paltry the benefits and how dreaded the guardians of these benefits may be, the amount of time it takes to get assistance like welfare, Social Security disability, Section 8, Medicaid, and food stamps is so great that who would not fear a cutoff? It is not as if a prospective employer commits to hiring you for a certain length of time. The employee could be fired in a week, two weeks, or a month. Then what happens? In many cases, it is possible that a whole new application needs to be made, and the money made in the short period accounted for. Of course, it is not impossible to get back on benefits, but in the meantime one risks oneself or a child getting sick with no coverage.

All social classes do a calculus of when work is needed, when retirement or vacation is possible, when a new job is in order, and so on. For the poor, this calculus naturally includes not only the income and benefits to be made by work, but also the costs of working, the loss of other income such as social benefits, and need, for example, of child care for children. Upper- and middle-class people often fault the poor for engaging in this calculus as if they should accept any job. But neither do middle-class people accept any job, and in fact in America workforce participation has fallen as many choose to stay home with children, go to school, retire, or go on disability. This choice is acceptable to the middle class, but not to the poor.

None of this is to say that creation of decent-paying jobs would not have a very positive impact and help change the current situation. However, it has been some decades since a major effort has taken place along these lines in the United States. Since in turn, lower-income people are well aware of the limited pay and status of current jobs as well as the lack of fringe benefits (made greater by the exclusion of part-time, temporary, and other less than full-time permanent workers) there is no apparent rush to the job queue. Here and there, formerly homeless people mentioned a desire for more work. Harry, sixty-six, in Los Angeles, for example, was getting retirement pay from Social Security but wished to work if he could, even at a position such as security guard. Two women in Portland, Millie and Sarah, both spoke of working most of their lives, but only being out of work now due to medical conditions (a common situation in all classes). But for the most part, subjects did not expect their social status or income rewards to change much if they obtained a new job or left social benefits.

SOCIAL BENEFITS AND SURVIVAL

American social welfare benefits do not and never were meant to bring people out of poverty but rather provide a bare survival living to recipients. Since the Poor Laws (brought over from England with the colonists), the American system has treated the poor harshly and with few material benefits. One aspect of our welfare system, for example, is TANF (Temporary Assistance to Needy Families) the successor of Aid to Families with Dependent Children (AFDC), the major program for poor women with children (although technically men are eligible). Assistance for a family of three (usually a mother with two children) ranges from a low of $170 a month in Mississippi to $770 a month in New York, with the median being only $427 a month in North Dakota.[7] This means that even based on the very low American poverty rate, TANF on average is something like a quarter of the money needed to reach the poverty level. General assistance welfare, a benefit never given by the federal government or in many cities and states, is the only benefit available to adults without children. It is provided by some states and towns, but has been abolished in many others. Among those areas where it has not been eliminated, it represents an almost pathetic attempt at aid. For example, in Los Angeles, general assistance is $216 a month, which would not begin to pay for a closet at LA's prices, much less someone's rent and other expenses. In Maine, general assistance is not cash, but a voucher system in which poor people receive a small amount of aid such as a transportation or food voucher. However, it may be superior in a way to California's system in that it can cover rent through a voucher. Still, this assistance rarely lasts for more than a short time, leaving newly housed people with the problem of how to pay the rent. It is awarded for a period until which it is believed that the recipient should get work, usually a period of months. Even more than TANF, general assistance would not make a dent in the poverty level.

Several social benefits that are more universal (i.e., that are given as a right of citizenship), can be more effective at preventing poverty. For example, Social Security pensions, disability, and unemployment insurance (all part of the Social Security Act of 1935) all can be important in preventing poverty or lifting people out of poverty.[8] Social Security retirement pays an average of $1,335 a month, hardly a fortune, but at least enough to put an individual above the very low US poverty rate.[9] Social Security disability, which has become the most important benefit for homeless people to get off the street and into housing, pays an average of $1,165 a month. Disability insurance covers a wide range of physical and mental disorders; however, it has a very high threshold to meet. To be approved for Social Security disability you must show that you have a condition that makes it impossible to work either permanently or for at least two years, with improvement unlikely. Further, as with Social Security retirement, the applicant must meet a test of work credits to be eligible. While the test is less than the ten years for Social Security retirement, it is onerous enough to exclude many potential clients. Very typically, the applicant must appeal several times to get disability. In 2011, according to a website about disability,[10] only 31.9 percent of applicants were accepted when they applied. An additional 11.2 percent did get aid when they asked for reconsideration. If they wait for an appeal (with a hearing wait time of 34.9 months) another 15.1 percent are approved for 58.2 percent approval.

Disability benefits are among the most contested federal benefits because of the desperate nature of people who are hurt, ill, or suffering from a psychiatric disability; they are increasingly excluded from other income programs. Since it is one of the few growing federal income benefit areas, the government protects as much as possible against too-easy approval. Attorneys and advocates support clients who are eligible to apply just as strongly. In fact, since I have met many poor people who have gotten disability only after a long struggle, it may be that the 58.2 percent approval rate is a little overstated. For example, if a client reapplies over several years, his or her chances may be much greater than that. Or it may be those with weaker cases fail to appeal.

Although a far inferior benefit in income than Social Security disability, many people, particularly the homeless and people with mental illness, find themselves with no choice but to apply for Supplemental Security Income (SSI). SSI has the same requirements as Social Security disability but it does not require the work credits. It is means-tested however, given only to those with low or no income or assets. Many very poor people have not worked on the books for a sufficient time to be eligible for Social Security disability. Mentally ill people are highly likely to be ineligible for Social Security disability because the onset of many disorders occurs at a young age and prevents the person from working for the time necessary to have Social Security credits. Congress created SSI back in 1973 by combining several old welfare programs—Aid to the Disabled, Aid to the Blind, and Older Americans Assistance—into a slightly less stigmatized program run by the Social Security office rather than the local welfare offices. It also raised the payments somewhat because welfare benefits in many states were so low. Another group eligible for SSI are those elderly people who do not have sufficient work credits to be eligible for retirement through regular Social Security payments (i.e., they do not have the ten years of work experience required by the "regular" retirement program Old Age, Survivors, and Disability Insurance or OASDI). This last category is rarer among the homeless compared with disabled people who receive SSI.

SSI payments are considerably lower than what people receive through full Social Security benefits from retirement or disability. They average only $559.45 a month.[11] The only bright spot here is that the state may choose to supplement the benefit. Maine pays a mere $10 supplement, one of the lowest in the nation. However, California is among the most generous, paying $171 more if you have cooking facilities and $255 if you do not. Therefore, in this example SSI would be less than $570 in Maine but as much as over $800 in California.

Income benefits are also important because they trigger medical benefit eligibility: Social Security retirement and disability come with Medicare eligibility, a program that, while imperfect in many ways, is still the best government medical benefit; SSI comes with eligibility for Medicaid, which while stigmatized and also full of problems, is relatively comprehensive in its coverage depending on the state. Subjects and most poor people are acutely aware of the status of their benefits affecting their health coverage. Another system that involved a few of our subjects is veterans' programs: eligible recipients can gain pensions from the Veterans Services offices and medical care as well as means-tested assistance for the poorest.

Benefits combined with housing subsidies amplify the effects on people because, as we have seen for those who get vouchers, normally the amount of rent would be capped at 30 percent of the individual or family's income. So, for example, if we take the averages given to people above only as a method of displaying the impact, we would see some of the effect of the subsidy assuming the benefit were their only income:

Retirement OASDI: $1,335 average rent capped at $400.50
Disability Social Security: $1,165 average rent capped at $349.50
SSI nationwide average payment: $559 rent capped at $167.70

Since, as we discussed, the rental market has leaped far out of sight of these prices, and generally does not come close to serving low-income people at 30 percent of their income, but is often closer to 50 percent of income, this is a big gain for poor people who do have housing subsidies. It makes people with any kind of subsidies more desirable for a landlord than decades ago.

The impact of income programs along with housing subsidies in Portland, Maine, shows that in this group there was a large impact of gaining benefits; all but two of those housed had obtained some benefits (two subjects had either TANF or general assistance benefit while most of the rest had disability benefits) and housing vouchers:

Bob: SSDI, housing subsidy
Charley: SSDI, subsidy for elderly/disabled housing
Elliot: SSI, but no housing voucher
Edgar: SSDI and SSI, voucher for housing
Ian: SSDI, housing subsidy
Jason: SSI, housing subsidy
Juan: SSI, housing subsidy
Louella: TANF, housing voucher
Miguel: working, housing voucher
Millie: SSDI, housing voucher
Nancy: general assistance, housing voucher (applying for disability)
Sarah: SSDI, voucher for transitional housing
Theodore: SSDI, voucher for elderly/disabled housing
Wynn: SSI, housing voucher

However, I don't want to overstate in any way the complex relationship between either income benefits or housing vouchers in getting out of homelessness. If one compares the interview subjects in Los Angeles with Portland above, we find only about 52 percent had social benefits (with more subjects working) and that only 43 percent had subsidies currently (although three other subjects had subsidies in the past that helped them get housing). The Los Angeles subjects' status is below:

Ace: some work, no housing voucher
Harry: retirement/social security, lives in SRO hotel
Christie: some work, housing subsidy
Shirley: SSI and work, supportive housing
Debbie: SSDI, housed now without subsidy (previously had Section 8)
Jeremiah: veteran's pension/SSI, housing voucher
Koki: some work, no housing subsidy
Cass: works, lives in non-subsidized housing
Laurie: SSDI, lives in SRO hotel
Leroy: SSI, lives in SRO hotel
Mindy: SSDI, housed without subsidy
Amelia: works, housed without subsidy
Mary: some work, was in transitional housing (subsidy)
Reggie: some work, housing voucher
"TRO": OASDI, housed without subsidy
Sally: SSI, housing voucher
Martha: works full-time, housing voucher
Rick: works, no housing subsidy
Violet: works, owns home (earlier had a housing subsidy)
Wally: veteran's pension, housing subsidy
Tyrone: veteran's pension, housing subsidy

There are many differences between the subjects interviewed in Los Angeles and in Portland. Importantly, as noted, the locale for many of the interviews in Los Angeles, though not all, was Skid Row, which has an unusual amount of low-income housing preserved from destruction. A number of the subjects above are currently in single room occupancy apartments, and others had been previously. In the immediate area near Skid Row as well, there are more lower-rent apartments available than in many other areas. Also, because several formerly homeless people are many years past homelessness, they have moved on and no longer need the same amount of help (for example, Violet, who now owns her own home, says she was greatly helped by a subsidy when she moved from homelessness to housing). Second, more of the LA interviewees are working. It is hard to know whether this represents a better employment picture in that city or means that some formerly homeless people have not been successful in achieving social benefits. Certainly, jobs like Amelia's and Shirley's as fill-in workers for factories are very rare in the New England area. Others like TRO and Rick are busy in acting careers, which is their dream and the reason they came to Los Angeles in the first place. Finally, there may be either a real or perceived difference in the amount of mental illness in the sample. Since mental illness is one of the more frequent pathways to receiving disability or SSI, it may be that Portland has a larger number of people in this category or it may be the numbers who are willing to go in and declare themselves as having a mental disability are greater.

It is important to know, particularly for citizens who think life on social benefits is easy, that quite a few people told me they had either rejected social benefits or at least had great ambivalence about them. Mary in Los Angeles "refuses to bother" with general assistance and other forms of welfare because she would have to account for the small sums she makes off the books (writing, teaching classes, massage). Reggie, whose work varies from playing drums with a band to selling nutritional supplements, has taken the same path. Three people interviewed, Sally in Los Angeles and Ian and Millie in Portland, told me they had been told many years ago they would each have qualified for disability benefits. Millie was perhaps typical in stating, "It was a hard decision for [me] because [I] considered myself prideful, and you know this [is] not who I am. I had to ask myself if I really wanted to sit home and collect a check." Although Social Security disability comes from tax money collected from payroll tax and is a right, many people do not think they should collect it.

On the other side are many who are still engaged in fights over benefits. Wally, the man whose severe accident left him quadriplegic, is still fighting his designation as a 50 percent covered veteran (he says because his unit was so secret) and is also in a suit against the swimming pool company, which has never settled with him despite the terrible accident. TRO, the actor, still smarts at the reception he received in Skid Row, where officials told him he could not get benefits while he had a smartphone. Sandy, the former contractor, regrets that when he worked and things were better, he did not pay in as an employee. Instead he missed eligibility for workers compensation and unemployment insurance. Now in very expensive northern Massachusetts, Sandy has to support himself and two children on $1,100 per month, including food stamps. "This is not . . . enough money to buy good food and to feed a growing fourteen-year-old boy," he complains.

IN DEFENSE OF SOCIAL BENEFITS

Over the last three decades or more, it has been fashionable to attack social benefits as wasteful, inefficient, promoting indulgence, and discouraging work. Even though the United States provides the fewest social benefits in the industrialized world, nevertheless conservatives (but many moderates and liberals as well) have led the political attack. Although occasionally dramatic as in the 1996 welfare reform bill (The Personal Responsibility Act), for the most part cuts have been gradual and cumulative, known mostly only to experts and the clients themselves. Fewer people are eligible for unemployment insurance in many states,[12] there are fewer units of public housing available, people are cut off welfare and food stamps, and states make eligibility for their programs far more difficult. In most cases, the arguments against cutting are fairly vague calls for compassion, a refutation of specific charges about a program, or warnings that if x is cut y will go up (usually hidden costs such as health care or work readiness). No major established group has been able to mount a full-scale campaign against the neoliberal assault and to say we need more, not less, social benefits. Liberals apparently feel that they cannot gain a majority of votes to a pro-benefits position.

Less than fifty years ago in 1969–1972, there was a bipartisan consensus that a guaranteed annual income was possible. Going back to the 1950s, authors and experts have raised concern about "automation" and called for economic and social changes that would meet the impact of new technologies. But as the society rhetorically repeats the "work" mantra, "everyone must work," in fact, fewer and fewer people are working, and in the next ten to twenty years there is a very good chance that millions, perhaps tens of millions of jobs, including white-collar ones, will go to the graveyard of history. Martin Ford's provocative *The*

Rise of Robots is just the latest in the many warnings our society has had about the vanishing job. [13] At some point, the worship of the work ethic by Americans on all sides of the political spectrum will have to vanish when the majority of people are no longer working.

But there is also a need to say the people who have benefits do provide for society as much as others. I have chronicled many formerly homeless people who are now spokespeople for their fellow homeless people or the poor or with political organizations. Others are active in social agencies and self-help groups. I have discussed participation in acting and music groups. Some of these are paid roles in which the subjects received small stipends, but many other roles are unpaid. Why are these time-consuming roles judged inferior to working a forty-hour work week? We know too that millions of people including our subjects engage in socially useful pursuits, not "lollygagging around," with their time. In Haverhill, Massachusetts, for example, one place where advocacy or political work was not prominent, we have Sandy working to care for his two children during the day, and particularly his special needs son who requires considerable help getting from one program to another. Billie, who during his fifties suffered a heart attack and stroke, is still quite active, including continuing an earlier career as a junk dealer. Lou goes to AA and NA meetings as well as counseling at the Veterans Administration and works out at the gym. He is also talking about going to the University of Massachusetts to get his degree. Ronnie, supported by disability benefits, spends a good amount of time with his two children and seeing his ex-wife with whom he is now on good terms, as well as going to therapy.

A broad defense of benefits must include the need for people who have been traumatized to have time to recuperate and be rehabilitated, physically and mentally. People who have been homeless, but also a wide range of people who have gone through traumas in their life, need a respite from stress. Why is it so threatening if people go to therapy or self-help groups rather than work? Why is doing theater or parenting deemed not as important a pursuit as working in a factory or in an office? Of course, the ordinary person probably does not even think about these choices, but it is effectively what we as a society have said: the only value is from work and working hard, and along with the old Protestant work ethic, it seems to be particularly praiseworthy the more we work and the less we really like the job.

It is ironic but the issues of the very poor and homeless may be the future for many Americans, at least in relation to work. New ideas such as a guaranteed income are going to percolate as more jobs disappear and more people drop to poverty.

5

COMMUNITY, SUPPORT, AND STAYING HOUSED

Most people who are familiar with the issue of homelessness have found over time that as hard as finding affordable housing and income support is, the problems of formerly homeless people only begin at the point a person or family is "placed" into housing. Below are four examples of the fairly routine developments that occur at times after a person finds housing.

1. Janice and her two children were placed in an old four-story walkup building. She made do though, until she received a letter from her local social service center telling her that they would cut off her TANF benefits if she did not explain how she received $200 as a present from a friend and why she did not report it. TANF is the family's only source of support.
2. Robbie is an older man who got his apartment with a combination of SSI (Supplemental Security Income) and a small amount in general assistance. He now has been informed that his landlord is raising his rent by 40 percent, an amount he has no way of paying.
3. Willie has been housed for three years and has been in recovery from alcoholism for slightly longer. He recently lost his parents in an auto accident, and has begun to drink again. He knows he is heading down the road back to substance abuse, but feels he cannot stop himself.

4. Lilli has now been housed for a year and a half after a long bout
   with homelessness. Her mother called this morning saying her
   father is dying, and she must come home to Texas from Massachusetts to see him. She has no money for the trip or time off
   from her job at a drug store. If she goes she most likely will lose
   her job, and possibly her housing.

These problems are routine in the life of poor people, and have no
simple solutions. Without doubt each of these calls for support; how
does one handle the social service office? The landlord? Your drinking?
Your family and your money? These questions are complex and strategic, but also highly personal and interpersonal.

Some people will jump to recommend counselors or social service
workers. There are several issues with this American propensity to pro-
fessionalism even though it is, of course, a well-meaning answer. First
off, a professional, unless you have an ongoing prior relationship with
one, is unlikely to be immediately available to you; depending on the
organization and its sponsorship (government, charitable, etc.), it may
well take you a while to make an appointment, and some of the most
knowledgeable workers are likely to have even longer waiting lists. A
second issue is whether from lack of knowledge of or faith in professionals, many poor people will simply not think of this resource. Third,
there are strong limitations on professionals due to the role of ethics in
what they may do. Perhaps in Willie's case above, they would be most
responsive to helping someone who wants to quit drinking, but in cases
one and four above, for example, they are rarely willing to help hide
money from the social service system itself or work around employers.
One would need a very special type of worker, and would always run
the risk of ending up in worse shape than when one began.

I suggest that the presence of a strong network in the community of
friends or contacts (and in some cases close family members) is probably a more likely source of ongoing support. These supports have the
advantages of (1) availability, particularly at off times such as non-nine-
to-five weekdays and weekends; (2) willingness to consider not only
ordinary but creative solutions, legal and extra-legal; (3) a reservoir of
more varied experiences and also scanning of the environment (maybe
there is a cheaper apartment complex than Robbie is in, for example;
perhaps another person who works at the drug store with Lilli can help

her strategize about her boss); and (4) in some cases, the ability to join the person at appointments or at other places where help and support would be useful.[1]

This chapter will situate the importance of community, along with housing and income, as key needs in the process of homeless people becoming housed. This is not to suggest that *all* communities or groups are positive. We will demonstrate the power of community organizations using two examples from this study, the theater group (which now also heads up a community museum) Los Angeles Poverty Department (LAPD) and the mental health organization and drop-in center Amistad in Portland, Maine. Interestingly, these are mixed organizations, having homeless, poor people, *and* some professional staff and middle-class members; neither lists "homelessness" as a membership criterion or was established for specifically that purpose. Although in some cases, a family member or a non-community friend has provided long-term help and support that may meet the needs of the formerly homeless person, generally it was more common in this study that community ties, both informal and formal (e.g., ties made on the streets or that are *not* rooted in formal charters as opposed to associations and/or groups such as nonprofit organizations that are formalized and that exist, at least usually, over a longer time) assisted homeless or formerly homeless people in staying housed.[1]

WHY IS COMMUNITY SO IMPORTANT?

A number of competing definitions of community have been offered since this word was first used. Some have focused on community as a geographical area, some on a group of people living in a particular place, and others have looked to community as an area of common life. It may be helpful to begin by noting that community can also be approached as a value.[2] As such it may well be used to describe a number of elements, for example, solidarity, commitment, mutuality, and trust. Community has also been approached as a descriptive category that incorporates place or "locality" and interest or "electivity."[3] Here community can be seen where people have something in common, and this shared element is understood geographically. Or people share a common characteristic other than a place such as a religious belief, sexual orientation, occupation, or ethnic origin that creates community through a common interest.

There are some problems with the broadness of the word "community." As Bob Fisher among others has pointed out,[4] community may represent prejudice, belligerence, and bullying as much as anything "progressive," as his history of conservative organizing shows. Think about the KKK or the "not in my backyard" movements against all types of people. Second, the way some talk about socially constructed communities such as the "gay community," the "Muslim community," or the "South American community" can be problematic. Many people who are gay or lesbian are not part of the activist gay community; Muslims have many ways of conducting their religion and do not always identify with their coreligionists as their primary identity, but as Arabs, Indians, Sikhs, Africans, or other nationalities; and South Americans too are more likely to identify as Brazilian, Chilean, Colombian, Peruvian, etc., rather than South Americans. Groups may be stereotyped rather than asked what it is they identify with, which is likely to be quite different and even variable.

Perhaps one can say the combination of geography and self-identity makes for strong community. "Skid Row" (though officially termed "Central City East" by the City of Los Angeles) provides a strong identifier for many people (though not all) who live in this area in central Los Angeles, such identity bound in social class and to some degree race (primarily African American).

How influential, successful, and sustainable a community can be has been described by Putnam as being dependent on the tolerance, trust, and reciprocity of its members.[5] This trust, tolerance, and reciprocity determines the level of social cohesion between members and reflects the nature and strength of social networks within the community. As Oliver and Cheff point out,[6] the fact that people live close to one another does not necessarily mean that they have much to do with each other. There may be little interaction between neighbors. The nature of the relationships between people and the social networks of which they are a part is one of the more salient aspects of "community."[7]

Social class plays a significant part in determining the strength of social networks. All research has shown that the lower the income of the community, the "tighter" the social networks. Ethnographic studies from Whyte to Liebow to Stack to Kornblum and more recently Wagner and Bourgeois,[8] for example, have shown low-income people (in a variety of ethnic and racial groups) rely on close bonds among both related and nonrelated people. For one example, while we often associate "going for brothers" or the use of "fictive kin" to describe nonrelatives in the African American community, I reported that there were similar dyads or more among non-black homeless people.[9] In this age of even less personal interaction and more impersonal technological interaction, the gap between face-to-face interaction between the poor and the rich has likely become even greater. The doctor, lawyer, and professor have far-reaching networks, nationally and internationally, that help their employment searches, careers, and status, but their networks are looser; they do not call upon a colleague for a hug or companionship or even a loan. Typically, neighbors in the middle class (and much more so in the upper class), do not know each other; if they do it is usually limited to the type of talk neighbors engage in "over the fence" or saying "hi" in a large apartment building. Being poor leaves one incredibly vulnerable. A strong sense of "peoplehood" and communal loyalty is more prevalent in poorer communities as security and protection against subjugation.[10] The less you know your neighbors or even people on the street, the more vulnerable you are to attack, but also thick networks serve to buttress mutual aid among the poor to survive through each week with limited resources. People on the street know which buddies might help them or even which storekeepers grant credit just as a mom in public housing needs to know who might lend her some peanut butter and bread or a few dollars.

For many homeless people there are survival benefits gained from close interpersonal relationships that are also central for survival. Sarah, sixty, a former homeless person in Portland, for example, notes:

"If I needed advice about something, I could go to someone in my
    neighborhood."
"I borrow things and exchange favors with my neighbors."
"I would be willing to work together with others on something to
    improve my neighborhood."

Wynn, a thirty-seven-year-old Native American man from Portland, also speaks very highly of the people he is surrounded by and talks about how supportive they are to one another: "We are a tight community—we will do anything for each other." We also have again Fiona (of

Portsmouth, New Hampshire) musing that "I have never seen a more caring, tight group than among the homeless."

Many formerly homeless people within our cohort continue to struggle with persistent and immobilizing poverty many years after they have found housing, sometimes throughout their life. The communities that face the most financial hardships suffer from strong social stigma by the public and, to varying degrees, by social welfare systems. Individuals who are not in traditional families and remain outside of social norms have long been viewed as the least deserving of the undeserving poor. Societal hostility becomes a unifier for this group of people and forces structured patterns of organization to survive in economic, political, and social welfare contexts that generally deny these people support and benefits.[11] United by similarities in their powerless, voiceless, and invisible positions, many people crippled by poverty seek out one another for mutual aid within the community. The norms of sharing food; cigarettes; alcohol; drugs; information about social services, benefits, and groups; money; and housing existed in many of the subcultures of the community of formerly homeless people who were interviewed.

A word of caution is always in order here. Extreme poverty and social policy hostile to poor communities has been very successful in crushing vibrant communities and social networks. The war on drugs, for example, and other changes in the 1980s onward have obviously weakened some of the social networks that, for example, Carole Stack found in her study of an African American neighborhood in the 1970s[12] (many of these changes have been documented in the work of William Julius Wilson and colleagues).[13] The ability of communities and groups to pull together is very uneven in the United States and has been severely affected by gentrification, the destruction of public housing, and decline in social benefits.

SOCIAL CAPITAL IN POORER COMMUNITIES

The term *social capital* has been among the most frequently used concepts in the social science literature. Social capital essentially refers to all nonmaterial capital people accumulate. A wealthy person obviously has sources of traditional capital in money, stocks and bonds, investments, real estate, and so on. But more subtly, the richer a person is in income and social class, the more they accumulate nonmaterial re-sources that intertwine with monetary resources. The middle-class or wealthy person has the education expected of them to be high class, literacy to read in at least one language, stylish clothes to wear, an accent and vocabulary that are acceptable, social skills to impress super-iors and those below, and so on. The accumulation of capital and social capital are obviously lifelong processes that begin in childhood social-ization.

The poor generally lack not only capital but social capital. Social service and rehabilitation programs attempt in various ways to make up for the lack. Although American service programs do little about mone-tary capital, internationally economic development at a village, tribal, or local level is very important. More often in the United States programs that provide clothes ("dress for success"), literacy, education, English, and even citizenship programs are examples of social capital remedia-tion.

In a 1991 article on homeless activism, Marcia B. Cohen and I sug-gested that tent city protestors gained both material and nonmaterial resources from the month-long protest.[14] Material resources consisted of housing (as the number of homeless offered and placed into housing rose), social benefits (general assistance benefits, Aid to Families with Dependent Children, Social Security and disability, veterans' assis-tance), and employment offers. But they also gained a series of nonma-terial benefits I will describe here: organizational attachment, access to people from higher classes, information, skills, and what we called *disal-ienation* (or what I call later in this chapter *resocialization*). Although the article's focus was on social movements, community organizations that are successful are very similar in facilitating these forms of social capital.

Before demonstrating the acquisition of social capital by poorer peo-ple, the limits of social capital need to be explained briefly. First, no amount of information or skills alone or resocialization or other gains can overcome the fact of poverty and associated life disadvantages. Only in conjunction with the kind of material gains that I discussed in chap-ters 3 and 4, at a minimum, can poorer people approach a level of success. In other words, we need to be clear that social capital is not a panacea. Second, one of the likely lessons of the 1991 article is that unfortunately even in situations in which groups obtain gains, material or nonmaterial, they can be short-lived and are often limited to the participants. For example, in the 1991 article we noted that an expansion in the provisions of general assistance by City Hall was very helpful to homeless people; however, after a period passed when there was little or no protest, as is typical, the city did not continue any expansion of this assistance. Similarly, when a downturn in activism occurred in the area, the organizational attachments, information, skills, and other benefits of the homeless or formerly homeless groups declined, and the key benefits accrued primarily to the *participants* in the 1987 movement, but not to their *successors*—people who were homeless or poor after this period.

POOR PEOPLE GAINING SOCIAL CAPITAL

Since poor people have no reservoirs of capital, they must bond as a group to secure social capital. Most people interviewed spoke of how different communities influenced them at certain points in their lives. Whether it was the solidarity found within the homeless community, the shared experiences in the recovery community (see chapter 6), the religious beliefs in the church community, or sharing resources in the poor community all were influenced in some way by being part of these communities. Many of the subjects relied on social networks of friends, companions, and family; some participated heavily in political action groups, self-help groups, church groups, clubs, creative groups, and social service organizations. As noted in the 1991 article, protest can certainly bring social capital to the poor in terms of concessions around housing, social benefits, and even employment; some employers came to "tent city" to seek potential job holders.[15] More commonly though, communities help homeless and poor people acquire the nonmaterial resources noted below.

Information

At first information may not seem to be a huge resource, but benefits and programs are so hidden from publicity and so arcane that collective groups and mutual aid that make programs of assistance better known to potential recipients of service are incredibly important. When Kelly declares, "It took seven years to be housed," she thanks the day she found a Housing First! Program in DC. This is unfortunately not unusual in the complex, labyrinthine world of our social service system, but affects many of our other bureaucratic systems such as employment in a complex society.

Access to High-Power Actors

When people are poor they are cut off from socialization and even superficial contact from the affluent and even the middle class. We noted in 1991 that such contacts are one result of the protest movement.[16] Additionally, in the groups outlined in this chapter, at least some of formerly homeless people made contacts with priests and ministers, social workers and administrators, and even occasionally job providers. Surprisingly, some of these friendships or acquaintances, particularly in the smaller areas such as Portland and Haverhill, could last. And even in Skid Row, there are numerous administrators, social workers, clergy, and others who take a strong personal interest in people. Life being unfair, it is often the younger, better looking, or smarter homeless or poor people who gain this attention (social capital even in terms of relationships is, like money, limited). Jason of Portland is a good example of someone who because of his activism and attachment to the resource center gained friends in higher places in the organization. When Jason "fell off the wagon" some years ago, a high-level official of the agency called the police and helped get him help for his addiction.

Organizational Attachment

As we shall see in the discussion of LAPD and Amistad, in addition to information and skills, poor people who are members gain strength from affiliation. Of course, people do not gain equal strength. But still there is a spillover effect that an organization has in the community. If you are a member of x group, which provides services to you or sees you in some role (e.g., a social worker or even a shelter attendant) perhaps the service provider has more respect for you if you are a member of a strong or popular organization. They may also have to anticipate what a negative action toward the person might bring by way of an entire group. Usually this is unsaid; many groups do not have need to police their reputation by actual conflict (the groups below, at least so far, operate in the community in a fairly collaborative manner, but they still can be expected to advocate for a member who is having a problem).

Skills

Some poor people gain specific skills from social movements or from organizational and community activity. The skill may be improved literacy, talking to the media, taking notes, organizing and conducting meetings, writing, and public speaking. Both LAPD, the theater group, and Amistad, the mental health drop-in center, promote the learning of many skills, the former because of the multidimensional roles of being an actor, and the latter because peers run the organization and must be prepared to be peer counselors or aid in the running of the agency (clerical work, kitchen duty, cleaning, etc.).

Disalienation/Resocialization

Some people are influenced so deeply by their community involvement and/or organizational or political involvement that it changes their life. We called this *disalienation* after Foss and Larkin's[17] usage in which individuals or groups reject their "socialization to subordinate positions." But the term need not be so dramatic; it can be more of a resocialization process in which people see their lives very differently. As Wynne and Edgar discuss below about Amistad, after years of involvement they began seeing some of the failures of the past (including their anger and machismo) but were able to change and replace such qualities to be leaders and peers at the center. Wally in Skid Row, Los Angeles, is another former homeless person who describes his new environment as transforming. Although Wally had participated in middle-class society and the military, he found the Skid Row environment helped him "find my sanity." He found more authenticity there than elsewhere. Immediately Wally became "Mr. Fixit," just doing anything he could—fixing broken bikes, helping collect material for people moving into apartments, and hammering broken things together. Later Wally became part of LAPD, LACAN, and the music group in Skid

Row. But these organizations seemed to follow his own self-transformation.

It should be stressed that there is nothing automatic about the positive results of community and resource gains. Poor people walk through a labyrinth of social and physical problems and barriers to any success. The individual must persevere through a host of dangers to survive, and the organizations and communities often must go through difficult times when they do not attract many comers. Old institutions based elsewhere—churches or AA, for example—will survive, but those newer and more innovative organizations and community approaches are often in danger of dying on the vine because of the terrific pressure of events in low-income areas.

However, the positive experiences of community resocialization for homeless or formerly homeless people does appear somewhat contingent on the availability of shared spaces where people have the freedom to explore trust, tolerance, and reciprocity with others. Several authors have explored the impact of intentional communities on positive resocialization in addressing social and cognitive deficits.[18] Recovery centers, religious establishments, and even prisons are some examples of intentional communities whereby resocialization may take place.

Whether due to the absence of role models, poor role models, or time away from societal norms and expectations, many people who have experienced homelessness describe a process of resocialization into "mainstream" society that takes place after finding housing. Whitley and colleagues depict the importance of rebuilding meaningful interpersonal relationships; many homeless or formerly homeless people report that previous relationships were often "dysfunctional," involving considerable exploitation or abuse. Whitley and colleagues describe how the relationships in a peer community setting were more inclusive and like a family. Here the community appeared to provide a facilitative environment for the development of social skills, social functioning, and social support. In this climate of peer support, decentralized decision making, and valued personal input, people learn that they are freer to be themselves and more responsible for those with whom they dwell and the place they call home. These experiences promote a kind of ownership for one's sense of personhood and place. Communities that place an emphasis on resocialization have been described by Whitley and colleagues as not only places whereby trust, tolerance, and mutuality are fostered in order to build relationships with others but as places where one can feel safe and prepared to "venture forth" into the world. Resocialization provides the individual with the skills that allow them to seek out positive and beneficial affiliations with others, which can in turn lead to acquiring resources as previously described.[19]

TWO ORGANIZATIONS (NOT ONLY FOR THE HOMELESS) AND THEIR IMPACT

Interestingly, but not surprisingly, studies of the homeless, even when following up on some subjects who are no longer homeless, tend to be stuck in the ghetto of homeless services. These studies are most often follow-up studies on how formerly homeless people have done in transitional or supportive housing, and if other issues are brought up normally the researchers do not move out of the social services for the homeless and the network of soup kitchens, clothes banks, service centers, welfare offices, and other places that constitute the nexus of where both homeless and formerly homeless people can be found. Because of the ability of this study to follow at least some formerly homeless people quite a while after they were homeless, I can present two groups of formerly homeless people even though they have nothing in their formal mission related to homelessness. Why might this be important? While no answers can be definitive based on one study, it can be argued that formerly homeless people integrate into society best when they are treated as normal members of society, freed from the stigma of homelessness. We suspect that there are many, many organizations in the community, especially religious organizations, but also political, business, labor, civic, service, and other groups that include some (or many) formerly homeless people, whether identified as such or not. In my book *Checkerboard Square*, for example, I discussed the community of people involved with politics, self-help groups, churches and ministries, and other normalized groups as well as social services. But dependent on the community, I can see the possibility of a labor union (farmworkers, service employees, others) with access to formerly homeless people and/or to businesses with special relationships to the formerly homeless (there are many small businesses that cater to the poor, where welfare checks are cashed or food stamps taken) and these small store owners often get to know people quite personally, even allowing people to "hang out," talk, and socialize.

This is not an argument that formerly homeless people can walk into *any* group or community institution with ease and integrate themselves. Clearly this is not an easy task for any poor person. Civic and neighborhood groups all have written or unwritten class boundaries; we will not find poor people at the Chamber of Commerce meeting, the Junior League, or the art museum opening. The two groups I discuss—the Los Angeles Poverty Department, a theater group based in Skid Row Los Angeles, and the Amistad Center, a mental health drop-in center and peer support organization in Portland, Maine—do have a set of social norms and culture that makes the presence of poor people more possible. While neither group would exclude affluent people, the manner of dress, speech, language, and habits of the members of these groups reflects their base in poorer people with, of course, a thin line separating members who may be working class (or higher) in the group.

The two groups are themselves quite different from each other. The LAPD, founded by John Malapde in 1985, came out of his efforts to combine art and a political orientation, but went through a number of changes over the years. It took years of work not only for the LAPD to create some successful plays, but for the organization to become well known throughout Skid Row and elsewhere. Its advocacy efforts have led to it becoming known among other organizations there—political, service, and civic. Further, recently the LAPD created a Skid Row Museum, a storefront that features exhibitions, performances, and meetings related to the 20,000 people living in the area and to its history.

The Amistad Center has its origin in the movement of families of the mentally ill, which arose in the 1960s and 1970s in the aftermath of deinstitutionalization. Originally called the Amity Center, the organization for many years was a modest-sized drop-in center and vocational rehab center located near the other social service agencies in a poor part of Portland. It too has undergone many changes, including a brief affiliation with Maine Catholic Charities; afterward, however, it grew markedly in size and services under energetic executive director Peter Driscoll, who was able to marry the consumer self-help peer-run philosophy with cooperation of the social service community in Portland—not an easy task. The Amistad agency now includes a hotline (called a "warmline") for mental health consumers, peer counselors at hospitals in the area, and a host of other services under its aegis.

As a theater group and a peer-run mental health agency, the two seem very different; however, both can be said to occupy countercultural ground despite some governmental and private foundation funding. Additionally, both have an ideology of inclusion that welcomes poor people. Because LAPD is centered in LA's Skid Row, its members are mostly poor, and its founder was himself an activist with homeless people going back to the early 1980s. Amistad grew out of the need to help the many poor mental health consumers who are not well served by the state agencies or private nonprofit counseling centers, which often tend to "cream" the crop of patients and use psychotherapy as a chief methodology. Instead, Amistad has embraced a "recovery model" for mental illness that parallels AA and the other self-help groups (e.g., it sees psychiatric problems as ongoing and always potentially overcoming the person). To recover, consumers must constantly work on their "issues" in self-help groups, other group activities, and participation in a variety of civic or recreational activities are all looked upon as positive. For many consumers, the commitment to recovery and to the self-help network at Amistad is lifelong. Over my nearly three decades in Portland, I observed that Amistad particularly served the very poor, among them the homeless. The ideology of inclusion and representation of the members (consumers and staff run all activities of Amistad, whether in its small restaurant or its many recreational activities or groups) usually ensures that low-income people are comfortable. No doubt some people always are uncomfortable, and do leave the Center; it is totally voluntary. In both organizations, some more affluent people (and sometimes poor people themselves) feel discomfort in the group, and may leave or just complain.

How do these groups work with their members and develop social norms that support very poor people, including the homeless and formerly homeless? I spoke with John Malapde and his codirector Henriette Bowers of the LAPD, and Peter Driscoll, the executive director of Amistad, about this. Additionally, nine people interviewed, as noted earlier, were members of the LAPD as of winter 2014–2015, and at least four were or had been members of Amistad (in this case, the representation is far smaller than Amistad's impact and relation to homeless people), both of whom I will refer to.

Undoubtedly, some features of each group may not be duplicated in every city. The location of LAPD in Los Angeles has some significance in terms of the presence of many people who came to the Hollywood–Los Angeles area to act, write screenplays, and perform other entertainment industry–related tasks. "TRO," whom we discussed earlier, is a professional actor who came to Los Angeles from New York City. Rick, discussed earlier, is also an example of a budding actor whose geographical location is tied to Los Angeles. Portland, Maine, while hardly as distinctive, has some features that may make it a favorable place; while a small city affording much face-to-face interaction, it was for years a center of activism for the rights of mentally ill people, and also of disabled and homeless people, generally as separate movements, but all have influenced Amistad.

Still, the techniques employed are hardly obscure or complex. LAPD as a group decided early on to have an inclusive strategy as its purpose and to represent Skid Row and the issues of poverty, racism, incarceration, and recovery through the eyes of the people there. As Malapde says, "[We] wanted to bring the skid row story to 'Normalville' [with] the lived experience of people in a critical way, one that would have a political or social policy significance." People are welcome to attend LAPD meetings and rehearsals, and essentially self-select the group. There are naturally people who have come and gone, and those who keep coming back. Malapde says that in his experience all interested people usually have some skills: they help in the process of script writing with their own lived experiences that they share; they may be good actors, but if not, they may sing or dance or have just one line in a play. Of course, expectations must be different for different actors, and what is a big development for one actor is not necessarily for the other. Bowers, during our interview, was very sharp in emphasizing that this was art, and they are now lucky to have an ensemble that would all recognize this. Bowers's point is that early on in Malapde and LAPD's career the emphasis was more on skits and political agitation. These types of performances are, of course, not without skill, but they are different from theater or art. Rather, art generalizes the experience of Skid Row or the people in it so that audiences can feel empathy and other deep emotions about theater. I watched the performance of *Red Beard/Black Beard*, an original play by Malapde taken from Japanese filmmaker Akira Kurosawa's *Red Beard*, a film highlighting a doctor's relationship with impoverished patients, and was quite impressed by the actors' skills in reenacting the Japanese film, which had some similarities to their lives, but also many differences. Certainly this play was hardly "agitprop," but a complex and artistic performance.

Interestingly, one issue that I thought would have arisen constantly was the personal havoc that homelessness and extreme poverty plays on people's lives. Having myself had some experience with attempts at engaging homeless (and formerly homeless) people in political and organizational life, I found major barriers including issues such as eviction, terrible housing conditions, loss of social benefits or jobs, addiction issues, interpersonal conflicts, and mental health issues, to name a few. Of course, the leaders acknowledged these, but seemed to have viewed the issues as manageable. Malapde said early in the group's life that because of his own activities in social services and also with Legal Aid, he was frequently in the role as a quasi-social worker in referring people to groups and assisting them with their problems. Here we see the provision of material resources for poor people. He noted that as the years passed, the strength of the group has shown itself in the ability of group members to assist one another. For example, Cass, discussed in earlier chapters, as a Skid Row activist who serves as a community organizer, is very capable of providing assistance to those who need it. At the time of my interviews, there were also at least three overlapping members of LACAN in LAPD who were also quite knowledgeable about services and legal issues. Like Amistad (below), a purist in democratic participation might find some holes in a seamless democracy. Each play performed by LAPD has a director or codirectors, and John and Harriet have assumed largely these roles. Hence the director/actor dichotomy is not open to question. Moreover, as in anything in our society, there are structural barriers to simply deciding he or she is going to be an LAPD actor. Actors are paid only for performances, and these are hardly Actors' Equity rates. Those who do sit on the sidelines or don't make the cut will not be rewarded that way. Even those who are actors or would be (such as TRO and Rick) find that they have to take other work and join other theater companies to meet their income (and other professional) needs, and even with these life is difficult.

Still, for the average member who is not necessarily planning a career in acting and who is usually (at least in the case of the people interviewed) supported by other assistance such as disability benefits, these limits are not a problem. Two of the nine members interviewed, Leroy and Laurie, have lasted approximately two decades with the group ("it has kept me sane" remarked Leroy). They have seen LAPD invited to the UK, France, Holland, Belgium, Bolivia, Nicaragua, and elsewhere. Mindy, when interviewed, spent several minutes discussing her experience traveling in the Netherlands, the first time this poor woman in Skid Row had been overseas. The group has won numerous awards in the last decade. But most important to the people I interviewed seemed to be its emotional impact on them. For example, Cass noted, "it helped [me] represent my hurt, the helplessness to voice all of my feeling I carried around in myself for years." To these members, the development in themselves was far stronger than only acting, but had to do with self-esteem and recovery, and political and social awareness of themselves as political actors.

Amistad, by contrast to LAPD, is a larger, more complex organization with hundreds of members and many more staff and volunteers. But what makes Amistad different from most service organizations is its focus on membership versus "clienthood." Those who join Amistad are owners of the program and participate in running the program. This means that when those we interviewed talked of Amistad, they meant not just a disembodied organization, but the friends and peers who make up the organization. Further, like the old settlement houses, and some modern clubs or fraternal organizations, the space and atmosphere of Amistad is organized around needs and likes of members, not a prescribed therapeutic agenda. Unlike other service agencies, a walk into Amistad will find members playing cards, talking, eating, playing pool, and working on computers, and so on, with no proscribed interruptions to have therapy or case management or other mandatory services. While joining Amistad as a member certainly sends a signal that one probably has a psychiatric history, there is no mandatory reporting of any diagnoses, or information or files kept on members.

The center has a shower, washer and dryer, lockers to rent, and phones and computers, and serves lunches six days a week. While the restaurant charges $2.00, one can volunteer there in exchange for food if one does not have money. Trips are organized for those who wish to camp, go shopping, or go to the beach. Driscoll, the executive director, notes that people in poverty (as most mentally ill people are) lack a car in a city that does not have much public transportation, but moreover

recognizes "the desperate loneliness" that comes from being poor, mentally ill, and stigmatized. The vision of Amistad is to provide "an open
and accepting environment . . . hence the basis of Amistad is Community." In my knowledge of Amistad over twenty-five years as well as
interviews with poor people, Amistad rates highly as a place to go and
belong, while some service agencies are felt to be intrusive and serve
agendas other than the needs of their consumers.

New members are particularly welcomed. A welcoming committee
is put together and there is an effort to make the new person known and
be greeted by all. Members can have peer advisors, which in some ways
mimics AA and other self-help groups' role of the sponsor. Members
are encouraged to volunteer, whether it is cleaning, doing laundry,
kitchen work, clerical work, or as peer counselors. According to Driscoll, people line up outside the door every day to volunteer.

Membership participation and control through votes of the whole
body or committees, however, do not mean that Amistad is totally "do
your own thing" or a place where everyone would go. One of the more
controversial decisions in recent years has been the creation of a "clean
and sober environment" in which drinking alcohol or taking drugs is
banned. This was a membership decision; given that so many members
have had substance problems, they are very unhappy with sharing space
with those who do abuse substances. A peer-run board administers a
process for those accused of infractions at Amistad, and suspension
from the program or even eventual expulsion can occur. This no doubt
may involve controversy, and as I discuss in chapter 6, the model of
recovery can produce some difficulties between members of the ex-
homeless community.

Like LAPD, the mission of the organization does not specifically
address homelessness. However, it has always been understood and
communicated by word of mouth that Amistad is a welcoming place
open to all. Louella, who as discussed earlier was homeless and new to
Portland, notes that initially she hung out at the places where homeless
services were offered specifically. She found the place to be dirty (blood
in the bathroom) and that the constant presence of addiction (such as
crack being smoked in the bathroom) repelled her. When she heard
about Amistad, she went there and was immediately struck by both staff
and members: "Everyone is so caring," she commented. She immediately began volunteering, and some weeks later, a baby shower was held

there for her (birthdays, weddings, anniversaries, and other occasions are marked here, and pictures of members grace the walls of Amistad). Some members, such as Edgar, initially came to Amistad after being thrown out of another organization. This welcoming atmosphere, the peer availability, a place to stay comfortably during the cold days of Maine's winter, and the referral to social services have all made Amistad popular with the homeless and former homeless, again providing material and nonmaterial resources.

Of course, those who use substances openly may have different feelings. There are also those who for various reasons drop out of activity there. Theodore, whom I discussed earlier, was an activist member at Amistad years ago, and still occasionally drops in and attends certain events. He did not describe at length his increasing distance from the organization, but my sense based on interviews conducted in the early 1990s for my book *Checkerboard Square* is that personality differences were the key contributor to his alienation. At that time, a rather "tight clique" of people controlled Amistad socially, and this alienated some other members. Of course, when members elect people, that does not always mean they are going to do a good job and be fair to all people. This particular clique seemed to alienate many members. Further, like LAPD, there are aspects of Amistad that may be criticized. While described as a democracy, its executive is not a member but a professional social worker, and while there is very definite input by members in selection of an executive and other staff, there is still a divide there. Part of the skill of staff is being good at reading members' opinions, and sometimes coaxing them to change them when major decisions are being made. If it is democracy, it is a very steered one in which most controversial decisions are subject to staff and director agreement.

Yet although, like LAPD, Amistad would not be for everyone, a large number of people remain as members for many years and see it having a transformative impact on their lives. At least for some people, the force of groups and peers can be more powerful than other modalities such as counseling, and for others these experiences are combined with counseling or therapy. Wynn, a formerly homeless person interviewed for the study, exclaimed: "Amistad is my real home—this is where I have learned to live indoors. When I first came to Amistad, I felt I did not fit into the community, because I wasn't mentally ill or drunk [but] I am a drunk and illiterate, I [do] have anger issues."

Wynn's quote leads us into an important discussion about what it is exactly that helps homeless and formerly homeless people stay housed when they are actively involved in such groups as LAPD or Amistad. We know that activists have more information available to them and hence more resources for help in times of need, as discussed earlier in the chapter. This process is important and includes not only getting leads from peers but information and strategy from those more experienced and higher up in the hierarchy, such as staff or directors. But perhaps an even more important thing is the resocialization aspect. Peter Driscoll put it well when he said that people with mental illness often do not have the greatest social skills. The onset of much mental illness is at a young age, at a time when other young adults are dating, going to school or college, and learning social skills. Those who struggle at these ages have not had time, Driscoll notes, to practice new social skills. They go from a casual relationship to having babies without preparation. They are thrown into adult situations—with landlords or even fights with friends—without having the years of practice. Driscoll sees the peer process as helping people learn such social skills. It is "part of the magic . . . learned citizenship that helps people really engage with others and society . . . to get on with their lives," he notes. Driscoll also links the learning of citizenship to the issue of homelessness:

> Take, for example, someone who's been living on the streets and he gets a place, [and] has [been] inviting his drinking buddies over, getting in fights with other tenants and not being a good citizen, not respecting other[s] that live there so the landlord kicks him out. He lasts [in the apartment] two weeks. We show people that you have to be a good tenant, a good citizen, responsible.

In other words, when people like Wynne and Edgar come to Amistad, they begin to be part of groups in which their actions may be criticized and their anger identified. They may be advised (or even engage in role play) as to how to handle a situation with a landlord or a welfare worker in a better way. I would suggest that LAPD as an intense group of twenty (or more) with strong norms of interpersonal sharing and reflection may have a very similar effect in providing feedback to members on their actions. This resocialization is not without contradictions or problems: Does such socialization locate all sources of anger only within the member? How are oppressive social forces that affect people interpreted? We don't completely know the answers to these questions (although see chapter 6), and it may well depend on which peers are present and interpreting behavior. At Amistad particularly, it appears that a type of therapeutic personality is promoted, with people able to be introspective, and even judgmental of themselves for past actions. Many of the LAPD members were also quite sensitive and drew on autobiography, often to share mistakes as well as accomplishments. But there may be some question about an emphasis only on "getting along" with landlords or other authorities.

Despite some questions about this socialization, we can see how involvement in these groups promotes integration of formerly homeless into their community. Both Skid Row and the Portland, Maine, service community are, despite their differences, highly therapeutic communities, with high marks for introspection. Skid Row, though known to citizens for its poverty and homelessness, is actually the "biggest recovery community in the country" according to LAPD (and others). The housed community prizes self-help groups and a positive recovery from the streets, substances, and other social problems. While it is hard to know whether all of Portland can be characterized this way, certainly the social work and mental health communities will share this ethos and they and other caretakers hold a fair amount of power in assisting the formerly homeless with all sorts of resources such as housing vouchers, getting into rehabilitation treatment, and other programs. The fact that veterans, even sometimes short-term veterans, of these groups can explain their issues and maturely react to the anger and frustrations of everyday life for the poor, will certainly be advantageous when they confer with therapeutic agents.

BRIDGING SOCIAL CAPITAL: ON THE VIRTUE OF MIXED COMMUNITY GROUPS

In his book *Bowling Alone*,[20] Robert Putnam stressed the importance of bringing together people from many different backgrounds to create an inclusive community where all people benefit from "bridging social capital," in which bonds of connectedness formed across diverse social groups leads to economic opportunity and inclusive democracy. This idea of "bridging" relates to bridging the societal gap between class,

race, and gender, incorporating the whole community as one entity and
not just the sum of its parts. Incorporating equal opportunity and par-
ticipatory engagement in all aspects of social, economic, civic, and political life is not dissimilar to the principles of the War on Poverty. Utiliz-
ing the idea of maximum feasible participation, Melish illustrates how
the concept of "bridging" class divisions is more beneficial to poorer
communities in terms of poverty alleviation, health, and education than
any other antipoverty strategy.[21]

Although I want to be careful about generalizing, the discussion of
these groups not identified with the homeless and not composed of a
majority of homeless people leads me to suggest some points that have
been rarely discussed in the area of homelessness: their communities
and political action and movements among them.

Most of the relatively small body of scholarship on homeless communities and social action ("tent city" protests for example) treats the
term *homeless* as a term without problems. We all know that those who
assemble on behalf of the homeless, join a tent city, or live in an encampment are as complex as defining homelessness, which is itself not
always easy. A careful reading of many studies as well as my own experience suggests that often what is termed *homeless activism* emanates
from a set of issues, not always from a majority of homeless people.
Some of this ambiguity became a central problem in the "Occupy"
movement in 2011–2012, when living on the streets became contested
between protestors and those who economically had no choice but to be
on the street. In fact, most times when people gather in any number
about the issue of homelessness, the assembly is likely to include actual
homeless people, formerly homeless people, advocates, social service
staff, and political activists who identify with the causes or demands.
Most times there is little reason to point this out, and the general tenor
of modern American "identity politics" tends to work against pointing
this out. Advocates or sympathetic politicos support the idea that a
crowd supporting "help the homeless" or "build housing for the homeless" are either homeless or just plain citizen supporters from undis-
closed places. But in fact, networks of former homeless people, advocates, social agency personnel, and political activists tend not to be
highlighted. I have often looked at pictures of some local crowds after
rallies of different kinds and it is not at all unusual to find a plurality of
service workers and political activists (sometimes both). I believe this is

true everywhere. It is almost kept a secret that people on the margin of homelessness, activists, and former homeless people, as examples, are very much part of any grouping.

What I am suggesting is that many observers and sociologists may be missing the very power of *mixed groups* to bring about change. LAPD and Amistad illustrate that diverse people can assist each other across lines of social class, gender, and (to different degrees) race and ethnicity. LAPD includes experienced theater directors, several people with growing theater experience, and a group of less experienced people. They include more poor people than not, but certainly some people who are middle class. The directors of LAPD are white, though most of the members are African American (Malapde says the racial composition has varied over the years). Amistad similarly includes director and staff, outside volunteers, and a host of internal volunteers and members. They vary greatly in education, work experience, and social class, although again the preponderance of members are closer to being poor than middle class.

This "mix" may be important because my experience in homeless political action suggests that when groups are homogeneous, and particularly lacking in social and economic resources such as the homeless, they may be handicapped by such conditions. First, almost all observers have noted the episodic nature of homeless groups, organizations, and protest. The very instability of life among the homeless (and ex-homeless) makes the daily task of meeting, phoning or e-mailing, leafletting, and other tasks very difficult. Quite often it is professionals or other middle-class people who take on these roles. Second, when a period is observed—one example is from the film *Tent City, U.S.A.*, which shows a period of activism in the life of the Nashville, Tennessee, homeless[22] —one sees the important role of professionals and volunteers in the process of action. In *Tent City, U.S.A.*, two ministers from a nearby church obviously were very instrumental in starting the organization of the tent city as a mini-community with its own meetings and services. When a flood suddenly destroyed the tent city area, the ministers themselves became disoriented and most of the (homeless) occupants of the tent city scattered. There are some actions the film further follows, such as the election of a homeless member of an advisory council, but again the reliance on the ministers' strategy is clear. Arguably the ministers were in charge throughout. Another film about homeless people, *Inside*

Life Outside,[23] while very movingly displaying the lives of seven or eight people who were homeless, also highlighted the role of legal aid lawyers defending them from eviction, who clearly played a large role in the tactics and strategies. Of course, I am not arguing that in no case are homeless or near homeless people able to plan for themselves, but most of the time, activism must be studied as a joint venture between poor people and allies not from the streets, but with some resources to offer them.

My point then is rather than being embarrassed that not all the players are "homeless" (most difficult of all is distinguishing the ex-homeless, who are often buddies of those people who are still homeless), the alternative is to embrace the possibility of mixed groups. Yes, it is difficult sometimes to work with people whose education, skills, and sometimes power may overcome the less sophisticated members. But this is true among any group including the poor and homeless themselves; often a particularly sophisticated person or persons with a great deal of experience or education can jump into the lead over the others. Most importantly, the "leaders" such as John, Henriette, and Peter must have a deep sensitivity about their advantages and powers and a commitment to provide all the power that is possible to those members who have never had the potential to rise as far professionally. Of course, the "members" in turn must have a deep and reliant trust in the leaders, or the leaders will be changed, either by internal means or often simply by members voting with their feet. Both leader and members must have the same objective, whether that is a set of plays that exemplify life at the bottom of society or a peer-group-led social club for those labeled mentally ill.

Mixed groups happen all the time and are hardly limited to LAPD and Amistad. Some service agencies and organizations and religious ministries are everyday examples, as well as many political efforts for the poor. Of course, service agencies are more middle-class (and even upper-class) dominated because their boards of directors are usually composed of higher-class persons. The day-to-day experience of a client or consumer is with mixed classes, but the structure and purposes are determined elsewhere, not only by their board but by united ways and other bureaucracies. In this sense, the less bureaucratic and more counterculturally oriented LAPD and Amistad may be seen to have a far better chance to have more equality than some other organizations.

Mixed groups may ultimately help with issues such as staying housed because they combine expertise brought by educated or skilled workers with peer groups who are up to date with developments on the street. While it is true that on some days in some particular cities, a social worker or case manager may be able to make a phone call to several landlords and find a place for a homeless person to live, the reality is that that hardly guarantees the long-term success of the person in achieving safe and adequate housing. Since this is likely an ongoing struggle, follow-up of housing placements not only by service agency staff (such as case managers) but by a combination of peers and volunteers or workers may be a best approach to keeping people housed.

Finally, we see that not every organization working with homeless or formerly homeless people need be so labeled. The stigma of homelessness is so strong, and as Goffman remarked, so "sticky" that it makes people distance themselves from the label.[24] I have in fact met homeless people themselves who reject this label. Given that over time—longitudinally—most homeless people do become housed and mix with average citizens—it is not a bad idea that group actions that include homeless and formerly homeless people have different labels depending on their purpose.

Even the best communities, however, cannot achieve much without the existence of adequate and affordable housing and other needs such as income benefits to the poor. In this sense, we must take care not to follow some of the communitarians in overemphasizing social capital only.

6

THE THERAPEUTIC ROAD TO RECOVERY

Exits from Homelessness

For most of the formerly homeless people interviewed, the road back from the streets was couched in the language of "recovery." Not everyone who used such terminology and explanation was literally recovering from alcohol or drug addiction or had a mental health problem (mental health recovery has increasingly adopted this language); some without these issues used this language along with some New Age influences (not surprisingly in California particularly). This chapter will examine this language and belief system, with its positive aspects and possibly negative effects. Additionally, as the question of whether homelessness might recur is always a concern in studies of the formerly homeless, I will discuss my own assessments of the people I interviewed and weigh their prospects for staying housed.

THE LANGUAGE AND ACCOUNTS OF THE THERAPEUTIC

In their seminal book on the American character, *Habits of the Heart*,[1] Robert Bellah and Richard Madsen contrasted several roots of Americans' language and social commitments including religion, civic virtue, and the rising therapeutic vision of American life. While they have been joined by other observers of American life, many people still associate therapeutic language and explanations with the middle class (or those even higher in social status), who were the original "clients" of psychoanalysis and counseling in Western society. However, it has been my experience that at least in the last two or three decades, a host of influences on lower- and working-class people has also promoted a view of life that stresses individual issues and ways to surmount personal suffering through an almost quasi-religious belief in "recovery" and an affirmation that a community, often a counter-community, exists to re-affirm oneself.

The influence on poor people in this book includes self-help groups such as AA, NA, and their many offshoots having to do with dozens of personal problems; therapists, counselors, and social service profession-als who influence people both through work with clients individually and their use of labels on groups of people; and also alternative organ-izations, including groups I profiled in chapter 5 (the Amistad Center in Portland, Maine, and the Los Angeles Poverty Department) and other political and religious groups that, while a bit more peripheral, do pro-mote acceptance of different religious, cultural, and social understand-ings of issues from a countercultural standpoint. While the methodolo-gy of Amistad or LAPD is group, the "takeaway" in recovery language is very individual.

Many people interviewed for this book spoke of *therapists and coun-selors*, *addiction* (usually to drugs or alcohol, but occasionally not—gambling was mentioned several times and issues of weight or spending as well), of *dysfunctional* families, *self-medicating* (the phrase originally from professionals indicating that the subject is coping with his or her serious problems requiring medication by taking drugs, legal or illegal, or alcohol), *self-esteem*, *post-traumatic stress* (a condition originally a diagnosis for veterans of wars, expanded to domestic violence, and now given to many survivors of serious abuse or circumstances in families or groups that produce trauma),[2] *enabling* (a term initially from AA for those who assist in the process of helping an alcoholic stay that way), and *healing* (although a more all-purpose word, it has gained currency in both mental health and New Age circles as a process of recovery and rejoining society). It was also of interest to note that many of the sub-jects discussed *bullying* early in their lives, *learning disabilities* diag-nosed usually later in life or retrospectively, and even *workaholism*, all terms that showed a good awareness of the language of personal issues in twenty-first-century America.

However, these subjects were not just parroting language or diagnoses; they used the terms correctly and with understanding. Typically, but only meant as a composite of different interviews, subjects often answered a question about their upbringing by noting that they were "from a dysfunctional family" characterized by abuse, poverty, drink, drugs, experiences of foster care, or some combination of the above. Generally, although the onset of their personal problems was different, in some cases occurring by adolescence or young adulthood, sometimes later, each spoke of "something snap[ping]" and experiences with drugs or alcohol or mental distress occurring. The "something" varied greatly from family issues to loss of work to abuse to death of family members, but set off a process that included homelessness, with an array of coexisting problems. The range of problems that set off this suffering varied considerably, and was usually not discussed as part of poverty or a lower-class life. Hence, as in professional speech and most public discourses about homelessness, the condition of homelessness was not usually discussed as a subset of poverty, but as an effect of personal or familial disorder. In fact, many subjects described issues of mental health, abuse, or substance use as a more "master status," as sociologists say, than homelessness.

Except for age—older formerly homeless people were less reliant on this language and therapeutic explanations generally—the descriptions crossed all lines such as gender, race, the city where they were interviewed (Los Angeles area; Washington, DC, area; Portland, Maine, area; Portsmouth, New Hampshire; and Haverhill, Massachusetts, area), and education. Martha, a fifty-one-year-old former student of mine at California State–Dominguez Hills, who is now a rehabilitation counselor in northern California, was very eloquent about the influence of both mental illness and drugs on her earlier life:

> [Most] of my problems in life including, a number of bouts of homelessness were in part due to my family history of mental disorders and [my] self-medicating them with pills. [The] problems were also exacerbated by my long-time husband, who also had a mental disorder, used pills, particularly amphetamines, and blamed all our problems on me. He [her husband] did not believe in paying the rent. He

would pay for pills or other things like gambling, and then blame me when we did not have rent money.

Martha attributed a lot of her problems to "developmental issues," which she eventually grew out of:

> By the 1990s when I was in my thirties I stopped myself cold turkey [from the pills]. . . . I think a lot of it was developmental issues, in my late thirties I began to look around and see how abnormal we [she and her husband] were. I went into therapy in [my] early forties, provoked by a very hard pregnancy. . . . I was on Prozac and Zoloft, neither of which helped, finally Zelaca helped me, and I spent two years in therapy before [my] coverage ran out.

Martha also traced the origin of her mental illness in how

> I could not get parents' attention so [I] sought it in all the negative ways.

Like Martha, who identifies as having a bipolar disorder, Bennie, thirty-three, a formerly homeless man in Portsmouth, New Hampshire, carries this diagnosis, although he has also been diagnosed in the past with depression and anxiety. Although Bennie does not even have a high school degree compared to Martha's college education, he was just as articulate in tracing his disorder. He too grounded his problems in his "dysfunctional family," which included an angry father who left the family and a mother plagued by disorders that he identifies with, saying, "I guess we have the same genes because everything that happened to me, also happened to my mother." He began to have "weird thoughts" in late adolescence and "took to alcohol to self-medicate." He had a girlfriend who became pregnant, had the child, and then left him with the child. He was twenty-one and made a suicide attempt. "At twenty-one I had no idea of how to handle a child," he says, and now he feels lucky that eventually the child was adopted by his aunt in Florida. The baby who shares his name has grown to be twelve, and Bennie sends him money and visits when he can. He will eventually tell him the history of his birth.

Like others interviewed, he has horror stories of illness and hospitalization, but also is very appreciative of therapists. He discussed one local hospital where he was on eight or nine drugs and had a variety of diagnoses. At one point, he ran out into the street with cars racing across, but survived this suicide attempt. He also cut his wrists during another seventy-two-hour stay at a hospital. His psychiatrist "fortunately" overruled the hospital's suggestion that he be placed in a state mental hospital. He describes himself as "very lucky," with his current and a former therapist who have helped him not only in counseling but in roles as case manager and advocate. Bennie's story does not describe complete recovery. He lives in a boarding home with a majority of alcoholics and does not see the local area as one conducive to his long-term health. He hopes to relocate to Phoenix, Arizona, where he visited and felt he would have better opportunities than in New Hampshire.

One surprise to me was how many African American and Latino subjects had seen psychiatrists and other mental health counselors,[3] and how many ascribed positive changes to the mental health system. Amelia, a fifty-nine-year-old Mexican American who is now active with LACAN, did not identify her troubles as mental or substance abuse in nature, but because she and her husband lost their jobs in the late 1990s. She had a second bout of homelessness in the 2000s, but has been housed stably since 2008. However, the premature death of her husband shocked her and led to her drinking a lot. She went "into therapy" and she quotes her psychiatrist as telling her she needed to "close up her life with her husband" and begin to "live a new chapter and start a new life." She attributes her activism for over five years in LACAN and her job and housing stability to the help of the therapist. She is a fill-in factory worker, and usually works a few days a week. Not only was I surprised by a middle-aged Latino woman going to therapy, but I wondered later how she could afford to consult one.[4] Mindy, the African American woman with neurofibromatosis described in chapter 2, similarly attributed much good in her life to her work with a therapist. The fifty-four-year-old discussed her childhood history of rape and abuse, which she has learned "not to dwell on" any longer, but "just accept." She has had many years of depression, even suicidal tendencies in the past. Her work in therapy has helped her "accept herself and love herself and keep wiping away the tears." For Mindy, a religious belief is not incompatible with a therapeutic belief; she said she has come to "love the Lord" as well as herself.

In the focus group interview in Washington, DC, most of those interviewed identified as having a psychiatric disorder, most commonly a bipolar illness. This included Johnny, a fifty-seven-year-old African American man, who is an electronic engineer, and lost a position after having "a nervous breakdown"; Jessie, a forty-eight-year-old African American man who once worked at General Motors; and Arnie, the fifty-six-year-old African American man who had been a federal security officer before succumbing to mental illness, discussed in chapter 2. All of these men found homelessness a huge shock; they came from middle-class or skilled working-class families. Each man fell from their origins and jobs into poverty because of mental illness. Johnny's fall began in his mid-forties as his huge time investment in work took its toll on his marriage and he became separated. He began getting increasingly depressed when alone, and then lost both his parents within six months. He had a "nervous breakdown," began drinking, "self-medicating" to cure the depression, and began calling in sick to work. He eventually lost his security clearance to work on government contracts, which still causes problems for Johnny in his career. Johnny sees his recovery as part of the success of counselors and self-help groups, but also the activism with the homeless groups and his faith in God.

Jessie sees his downward turning point as his mother's passing away. He says he had a "manageable alcohol problem but an undiagnosed mental illness." He, too, was self-medicating with booze, and also gambling. He was diagnosed as having a bipolar illness in 1990. Jessie also proudly mentions that he has been through anger management training. As is part of the "recovering" paradigm, none of the men—Arnie, Jessie, or Johnny—sees himself as fully recovered, but as "work in progress." Johnny wrote in the DC homeless paper about "trying to make it still. . . . My tools are coming together. . . . I want to continue my education." Arnie notes that he has finally forgiven himself for the failures that led to his divorce and his loss of his house.

Two interviews with African Americans in Los Angeles, Reggie, forty-eight, and Mary, also forty-eight, suggest some of the New Age mix in some of the interviews.[5] Reggie, a man with long dreadlocks who says he has been housed for six years, told of a long history of wandering, arrests, and drugs including living in downtown Venice, California, a countercultural haven that is a mix of poor, homeless, and middle-class people living on a beach well known for drugs. Reggie talked of his "powerful insights" into life, which led him to Islam, but later into studying all the religions, and seeing similarities in all of them. At one point Reggie lost me a little in using geometric images and the unified and string theories to illustrate where he had come to spiritually and why it might be time to wander again. Reggie says he earns enough through serving as a drummer in several bands and selling nutritional supplements and organic teas and coffees to survive. It was hard to gauge his income.

Mary, who frequents LACAN meetings[6] and has a long list of political involvements, also speaks of living in a large communal setting where she embraced vegetarianism and a "Hebraic cult." Like Reggie above, she also claimed political commitments, but their conversation was influenced by countercultural thrusts. When Mary had a baby, she came into conflict with her separated parents, both middle-class professionals, and was sent into the mental health system. Eventually her mother took her child. Mary, unlike almost all the others interviewed, expressed a strong dislike of the mental health system. She admits being diagnosed with all sorts of problems "including bipolar disorder and schizophrenia." But she rejects the diagnoses and believes that most of the trouble she has had, both with police and psychiatric authorities, was a result of her political and other beliefs. She called attention to what she saw as "a larger conspiracy to take black babies away from their mothers," which occurs daily. Mary, housed for twelve years, gets by on a combination of writing, selling poetry, doing massage, and teaching Japanese massage. As I will return to later, I was concerned about Mary, because her refusal to accept any diagnoses has meant that she does not receive any benefits including disability, and her housed situation could be precarious based on her low income.

Generally though, most of the subjects had gained a degree of stability from their roads to recovery. The road has many positive components: certainly a spiritual awakening, an introspective ability to reinterpret different aspects of life, a new language shared with both professionals and a growing group of like-minded people who are not professionals. It had some economic gain for the many subjects who have secured disability benefits and some who obtained other benefits as well through therapists, case managers, or advocates. The proclamation common in LA's Skid Row is that it is a "recovery community," echoed by Cass (see chapter 2); and Harry, a sixty-six-year-old African American longtime resident of Skid Row whom I interviewed, provides a counter discourse to the negative views of the area. It is quite interesting since passing visitors to this area often just see the large numbers of homeless people camped on the street and often comment (whether accurately or not) about addiction and mental illness. In fact, the majority of those who *live* in the SROs and also nonprofit residences of Skid Row (as opposed to those who camp out on the street) is very likely people who are currently or were in various recovery groups. Finally, recovery language and identification does provide a commonality and even arguably a culture, if you will, that crosses conflicting lines of race and gender, and to a degree social class among people who have suffered from different difficult issues, and now can accept each other.

Yet the culture or perhaps even ideology of recovery, while so valuable to many people, is not without its contradictions, which I will move to next.

SOME DIFFICULTIES WITH RECOVERY BELIEFS

There are some conflicts between the recovery discourse and some of the opinions of the subjects interviewed, and the discourse of homeless leaders and advocates usually expressed. Mostly these remained latent, although a couple of subjects did take them further. One is the possibility of separation and distaste between "recovering" people and those people who use substances or do not appear to be acting to resolve their other personal issues. Another area of conflict is how the individualistic discourse of therapeutic change contrasts with earlier discourses (similar in ways to the discussion in Bellah and Madsen)[7] and other beliefs about fighting homelessness that are grounded more in political, economic, and sociological theories. In other words, should the discussion of homelessness (or poverty) be centered in more group identifications such as social class, as advocated by many people who support the causes, or should homelessness or other social problems be seen as individual problems such as drugs, alcohol, and mental illness? In the traditional discourses of "republicans" and communal discourse, Bellah and Madsen would criticize the individualist therapeutic discourse.[8] Yet today the discourse of recovery is far more ingrained than older American discourses.

On one level, a number of subjects expressed distaste about some fellow residents. Shirley, a fifty-two-year-old white Los Angeles resident of Skid Row, opined, "I don't like Skid Row [anymore] with so many drugs [around]. If you walk around you will see more than a little weed and even crack in front of your eyes." Sarah, a sixty-year-old formerly homeless woman living in Portland similarly declared, "I try to avoid [street where shelter is] and [the street where the resource center is] where homeless [people] are—too many drugs and too many unsavory characters."

But a few subjects went further, supporting policies that were often opposed by homeless advocates. Millie, a thirty-six-year-old woman from Portland who was fairly recently housed, not only suggested her own substance abuse problems characterized everyone on the street, but agreed with a recent city policy to move people more quickly out of the major city shelter:

> All of my homelessness is due to my addiction issues. And I believe that most people's homelessness is due to this as well. I think it's wonderful that they [City of Portland] have [sic] implemented a new rule that clients have to be looking for housing in order to stay at the shelter. I [think] there are some people that chose to spend their whole check on drugs and alcohol.

Of course, many citizens might well agree with Millie's overgeneralization of substance abuse causing homelessness, and many of them would also be glad to move as many homeless people as possible out of the care of the city.

However, over the years most advocates and homeless activists have opposed a push to remove people from homeless shelters before large-scale housing and other services are available to people, arguing that this "crackdown" would only lead to a revolving door of people being unable to get shelter and simply returning to living on the streets. While no one opposes the idea of shelter staff and social workers speaking with and voluntarily planning for housing with shelter residents, if these efforts are mandatory and do not include housing, such efforts are strongly opposed. Millie's comments (like Leroy's below) contradict the goals of "Housing First" advocates who believe people can recover best in normal settings and that recovery can best be undertaken *after* being housed rather than the older view that society should wait for people to get off alcohol or drugs or recover from psychiatric problems first.

Leroy, a fifty-five-year-old formerly homeless African American resident of an SRO for many years, also voiced a dissident note when I spoke with him in Los Angeles. Like Millie, he tended to use his own experience to justify policies fought by advocates. After giving "thanks [to] the police and Jehovah" for getting him off drugs and the street, he suggested that he had hit "rock bottom and realized [he] was a crack addict."

> I feel maybe it is good that the LAPD (Los Angeles Police Department) is cleaning up downtown. . . . So many people in Skid Row do not take advantage of the housing there is; [they are] lazy and do not want to give even some of their money to rent [and there are] rooms available.

Here Leroy is referencing Los Angeles's so-called Safer City Initiative (SCI),[9] which throughout the last decade has led the LA Police Department to conduct thousands of arrests of residents each year through a "zero-tolerance" policy that has led to turnstile justice for many poor people accused of loitering, jaywalking, graffiti, and other formerly "quality-of-life crimes." Leroy reasons that since his own arrest for crack acted as a sort of "tough love" deterrent to his drug use, other residents needed this kind of discipline to change their lives. This would certainly put him on the side opposite to advocates for the homeless and poor.

Yet even advocates for the poor who were interviewed here used some of this logic in their own cases. Dwayne, a homeless advocate from Washington, DC, discussed in chapter 2, said,

> I got lucky when I was arrested . . . because there were no public defenders, and I had to be given a private attorney. [Due to this negotiation with lawyer] they let me go. I had to go to a shelter and they [the court] set up several conditions; one was to have mental health treatment.

Of course, Dwayne's comments are understandable as a person who faced jail, and who is now grateful for having mental health treatment for what he considers a longtime psychiatric problem. Still, like Leroy above, his comments give some pause as to policy about mental health and homelessness, and whether advocates should always support such arrangements. Tyrone, an activist and advocate with LACAN discussed in chapter 2, is still another who praised an agreement for him to get treatment. Arrested for selling drugs to an undercover policeman,

> I was given a nine-month [term], but [the] judge was fair. He agreed to suspend a five-year sentence if I did this [sign an agreement] and then went to rehabilitation. The toughest part was jail, once I entered rehabilitation; I had already stopped so it was not so bad. I also paid restitution.

There is, of course, a line somewhere between individual agreements made between officials and those who are poor and homeless or suffering from substance use or mental health issues, and the imposition of forced treatment. There is also presumably a difference in what advocates propose and what attorneys or other representatives may negotiate.

Still, a clash in LA's Skid Row over the possibility of a new bar and restaurant being located in Skid Row may clarify some of the emerging tensions. In December 2013, a number of protesters marched against the plans of a nonprofit organization, the New Genesis Apartments, to allow a storefront restaurant serving beer and wine (along with food) within the same complex (many of these organizations cannot make ends meet without this type of arrangement). While this process was, according to the *Los Angeles Times*, "normally mundane," suddenly city license authorities were challenged.[10] Some protesters chanted "No Wine, No Beer, Not Ever, and Not Here." Protesters appear to have wanted no temptation for those clients involved in New Genesis who had alcohol or other substance problems. Although they seemed to have backtracked a bit after the license was denied,[11] stressing populist issues of gentrification (which they argued had developed too many high-end bars and restaurants flooding the neighborhood) and offering in one protester's words "a diversity of uses," including restaurants more available to the less affluent, the point was mostly taken to be the opposition to bars. As the supporters of the bar noted, "people on Skid Row can get booze anywhere," and they noted that San Francisco and New York City had approved similar restaurants in "homeless housing projects with no trouble." One Skid Row man who went through recovery was quoted in support of the project, and one businessman claimed that a majority of residents favored the proposal.[12] The zoning administrator, in fact, said the decision could be reversed if proof of support from "affected residents" is offered.

While on the one hand, the success in stopping the bar was a victory of sorts for community organizing, it was not backed by most of the organizations in the area. To some extent, the idea of controlling bars and drinking may seem a distant objective these many years after Carrie Nation and the Prohibition movement, and indeed there are countless bars and other access points for booze in the downtown LA area. Some of this was confirmed to me by a leader who said that the members were split on the issue and hence no position was taken. But it also raises the question as to whether such strategies are the most important in fighting homelessness and poverty. Many issues are present in Skid Row, as elsewhere, and housing is usually chief among them. Issues of social benefits, jobs and income, and the police intervention in people's lives tend to be seen as more important to most advocates and activists than prohibiting alcohol or drugs.

Some writers have proposed a merger of anti-addiction treatment and more progressive politics,[13] but it seems to me that such a marriage is difficult at best. While recovery can certainly be a group or collective process, which the work of the Amistad Center (in chapter 5) suggests, this does not mean the focus moves very far to socioeconomic and sociopolitical issues. Why people take drugs or drink is rarely discussed outside of their individual circumstances. The high number of people using substances in poor communities is in fact often denied, replaced with populist notions that it is only enforcement of drug laws that leads to the large numbers of poor people in prison or jail for drug charges.[14] In fact, some of the Los Angeles groups such as the LAPD theater group have promoted to some extent racialist ideas about the crack epidemic, suggesting to a degree that it was a conspiracy (see *Agents and Assets*, about the CIA role in the Iran-Contra Affair and other evidence).[15] Similarly, issues of mental health are almost never politicized or viewed as potentially political as they were in the 1960s and 1970s when radicalism first came to the mental health field both among practitioners and patients (see journals such as the *Radical Therapist*, and groups such as the Mental Patients Liberation Front). It is a view of most interviewed that mental illness flowed through genes or perhaps family dysfunction and was not a social issue for society.

Further issues of housing, jobs, income, and social benefits stressed by homeless advocates and activists were not mentioned by most of the subjects interviewed. To be fair, I did not ask these subjects for their political opinions about homelessness. Some may in fact have assumed that I was aware of them by virtue of their associations with different groups or some labeled as advocates. But these numbers (of advocates) were still not a large percentage of those interviewed, and I often find issues discussed in a long interview, whether asked directly about them or not. Rather it seems, as with many Americans, that the answers that "recovery" and even New Age concerns provide are far more hospitable to subjects who searched for answers to their difficult lives. These are answers that are non-blameworthy, and as importantly, provided continuing identifications in their lives. To be "recovering" seemed to have status in the community, whereas being a poor person, a welfare recipient, an unemployed person, or other potential roles stemming from low social class may well have seemed more stigmatizing. Interestingly, some people were in groups that may have focused on poor people (like LACAN) but it seemed less essential to subjects to explain or tell a story about this stance than their personal links to substance use, mental health, or other personal battles. There are some exceptions. Jeremy, an older African American male who goes back many years in a variety of social movements such as civil rights and the early days of LACAN and the homeless movement, spoke more of activism over the years. Although I believe he has own personal problems, he did not emphasize the issues at all. But this was quite unusual in this study. It may be of interest to contrast this finding of a sort of depoliticization of some of the homeless in contrast to many of my interviews in *Checkerboard Square*[16] conducted in the early 1990s and some of the other treatments of homelessness around that time.[17]

It may also be the case that there is not only something about the therapeutic experiences (such as we saw in chapter 5) that obviously appeals to recovering people, but that homeless people without such labels may be more likely to go back to their lives without remaining very well known to either homeless activists or social agencies. As noted in chapter 2, only nine of fifty-one people interviewed did not disclose some form of mental illness or substance use. It is difficult to know because of this relatively small sample, whether this finding bears a true relation to what is a very high incidence or, consistent with many of our arguments about statistics about mental illness and substance use among the homeless, it has oversampled people with such issues.[18] If this is the case, it certainly would be interesting to try to sample more non-affiliated people (such as was true among the Haverhill-Portsmouth area where four of eight did not have mental illness or substance use problems) as opposed to those who came more from group identification in, for example, Los Angeles and Washington, DC. This will be a difficult issue to untangle; the less affiliated are by definition harder to find and to interview.

WILL THE PEOPLE INTERVIEWED REMAIN HOUSED?

One question that most service providers and workers will ask, if not others, is how many of the fifty-one people interviewed will remain housed in the future years. This is an important question because, as I have noted throughout, most homeless people are "episodically" homeless, not homeless forever, but on the other hand, not necessarily housed forever either. The constantly changing nature of low-income housing supply (usually dropping in number in most cities) as well as the fluid nature of the economy, particularly the low-income economy, makes change constant. In addition, if one prognosticates one must consider the personal issues the subjects had or have and the support the subjects have (or do not have) as well as the overall changes in the economy.

Though I lack a crystal ball, I thought it would be helpful to both note what criteria I found most helpful in evaluating subjects' future chances and make some general predictions. Of course, the best answer would be another study that follows up in perhaps two or three years and then five years to actually see what the realities were.

Generally, I found four categories of knowledge helpful in organizing my view on the subjects' likelihood of staying housed. This is not to say that there are not others equally valid, but whose knowledge I did not feel that I had (a complete housing analysis would be good for example).

Age

Although there are homeless people of all ages, the usual entry points into homelessness are much more likely to occur at a young age. Like many issues and social problems ranging from mental illness to substance use to crime, the impact of adolescence and early adulthood is a significant danger point for difficult personal outcomes. Additionally, many older subjects commented on age as a definite barrier to being homeless. Theodore, forty-eight, and Elliot, forty-six, two men who had been homeless in Portland back in the days of "tent city," cited age as significant in their housing situation. Theodore, a disabled man, says "it is not so easy living outside with my arthritis; when I was younger I could do it easily, not anymore!" He also cites his relationship with a woman whom he wants to marry as another factor. For Elliot, "it become pretty difficult [for me] . . . if you want to have a family [to be homeless], and my girlfriend is expecting a baby." Charlie, a formerly homeless man who was fifty-nine, put it the following way:

> Once you get to a certain age in life you don't bounce back like you used to, you get tired of waking up looking at your knuckles or face and you think, "What the hell happened last night?"

So both aging and vulnerability on the one hand, and the possibility of family ties on the positive side (and therapy dogs too! As both Wynn and Edgar explained, they had gotten close to their dogs over the years) begin to make getting housing seem very necessary. This, of course, is not to say that none of those who are older will become homeless, however.

Length of Time Housed Successfully

As in all of life, nothing predicts the future better than one's history. I was more reluctant to predict a safe future for those people interviewed who had been housed for a year or less; while on the other hand, those who had been housed for many years seemed a much safer bet, even in terms of economic and social uncertainties. Unfortunately, I was unable in a snowball sample to control this variable; I interviewed individuals housed only for two or three months, on the one hand, to seventeen years, on the other hand. For the most settled in the group like Violet (seventeen years) and Debbie (fourteen years), the story of their home-lessness was definitely remembered, but long past. At the other extreme, Millie and Bennie (both two months housed) had hardly transformed to "housed" people totally. In some cases, transitional-type housing may have left ambiguous the role of being "homeless." But also length of time housed for some led to accumulation of resources over the years. Violet had purchased a home; Debbie (above) and Paulie, a fifty-two-year-old woman from DC (also fourteen years), for example, had obtained college degrees, but even those who did not have such resources, those like Amelia (eight years) or Cass (twelve years) were likely to have had more standing either in voluntary groups (like Amelia) or at workplaces (like Cass).

Specific Economic Standing (Work, Benefits)

Here I must make my criteria clear in terms of expectations of low-income people. As noted in appendix I, few of our subjects were from high-income backgrounds, but rather were from families usually of working class or below. Outstanding outcomes such as Fara and Cass's levels of education and social service positions, Violet as a paralegal with a bachelor's degree or would-be social workers like Bob and Debbie constituted only a fifth or so of the group. I must evaluate income-generating abilities along a line of stability like good work income, or in the case of benefits, those such as Social Security disability or retirement insurance that has a good chance of not being cut or providing enough income (and medical care) for bare stability. Most of those who can be regarded as stable were those with such benefits or with benefits and a combination of small stipends from advocacy or service groups. Most of their jobs were lower paying—Shirley and Amelia as fill-in factory workers, Miguel at Dunkin' Donuts, Wynn as a janitor—or were off and on, such as Reggie playing drums and selling supplements, Mary teaching massage and writing, Laura doing bookkeeping work in the spring, and Billie selling junk. TRO and Rick were actors who seemed to be stable at the time they were interviewed, but may not always be employed. I tried to consider the rough amount of income generated by both jobs and benefits, though I had not directly asked this question. Generally, this was not a criterion that greatly boosted the chances of most of the subjects.

Personal Problems' Apparent Salience

The widespread nature of mental illness and substance use in this sample suggested that I needed to assess at some level the subjects' likelihood to remain sober or stable. Again, I did not conduct the interviews in a clinical manner, nor did I ask about the amount of alcohol or drugs consumed at the current time or assess how the interview data presented the subjects' mental health except in several extreme cases. Rather, here I had to use my judgment of age, years housed, benefits, and work generated in conjunction with the life histories of the subjects. Some stated no histories of mental illness or substance use. Most others, although not everyone in the sample, discussed recovery groups or the process of treatment or recovery, and I accepted the statements of the subjects generally as accurate, although of course never controlling of the future. Here as an opposite of the three above, most subjects appeared to be fairly stable in recovery groups or support systems.

Based on these factors, I rated twenty-six people (about 51 percent) as highly likely to remain housed. Seventeen people (a third of the subjects) I rated likely. Here the distinction was that I would (if I were a betting man) bet on the first twenty-six but would be a little more cautious with the next seventeen. Finally, there were only eight (15.7 percent) whom I felt were uncertain, and could go either toward stability or homelessness. See table 6.1 for the names of the subjects.

Some of my judgment is apparent in looking at the median ages and time off the street placed next to each name. The Highly Likely category had a very high average age of 55.5 years old while the Likely category was nearly a decade younger (46.5 years old). The Uncertain was only minimally lower (45.1 years). However, the sharpest difference came in the length of time the subjects were housed: the Highly Likely group had a median of seven years housed, the Likely only one year, and the Uncertain only three months.[19]

In general, I was cautious with some of those who were recently off the street. Albert, thirty-eight, in Los Angeles, for example, was soon to lose a stipend he had been receiving and while he is educated with a BA and seemed smart, both conventionally and street-wise, he had only been housed for a while and with an uncertain roommate situation. Dora and Dick, the middle-aged couple in Haverhill who were very happy with their housing, were still housed only briefly (seven months)

Table 6.1. Judgment about Future Homelessness (by Subject)

Name	Age	Time Housed
HIGHLY LIKELY		
Amelia	59	8 years
Arnie	56	4 years
Billie	62	1 year
Brian	60	8 years
Cass	64	12 years
Debbie	57	14 years
Dwayne	40	8 years
Edgar	37	3 years
Fara	44	1 year
Harry	66	1 year
Ian	57	4 years
Jason	61	2 years
Jeremiah	58	20 years
Johnny	57	7 years
Kelly	52	5 years
Leroy	55	14 years
Martha	51	20 years
Mindy	54	14 years
Paulie	53	14 years
Ronnie	47	11 months
Sandy	59	1 year
TRO	63	1 year
Tyrone	63	6 years
Violet	41	17 years
Wally	49	5 years
Wynn	55	3 years
LIKELY		
Albert	38	1 year
Charley	59	10 months
Christie	32	3 years
Dora and Dick	55–56	7 months
Fiona	62	2 months

Name	Age	Time Housed
Jeremy	66	7 months
Jessie	48	7 years
Louella	29	5 months
Louie	54	1 year
Miguel	30	2 years
Nancy	30	2.5 years
Reggie	48	6 years
Rick	27	1 year
Sarah	60	11 months
Shirley	52	1.5 years
Theodore	48	3 years
Tillie	53	Unclear
UNCERTAIN		
Bennie	33	2 months
Elliot	46	3 months
Juan	51	9 months
Koki	38	2 months
Laura	57	Unclear
Mary	48	12 years
Millie	36	2 months
Sally	52	3 years

and while they seemed very confident in their treatment situation (for mental illness) both had seen some recent psychiatric setbacks. In addition, one issue not discussed is that three of these subjects had quite serious medical conditions that emerged—Fiona, sixty-two, in Haverhill, Jeremy, sixty-six, in Los Angeles, and Tillie, fifty-three, in Washington, DC. Although not a major subject of studies of homelessness, these issues could get in the way of each of them staying in their current housing. These examples suggest my cautions in the Likely category.

The Uncertain category stood out at least in this particular sample in their newness to housing and/or their uncertain personal stability. Bennie, thirty-three, of Portsmouth as noted, while in a boarding house for a few months, did not regard himself as stable yet, and was hoping to save money to go to Phoenix. Several of these subjects were difficult to fully interview because of some psychiatric issues, particularly Juan, fifty-one, in Portland, and Laura, Michelle, and Sally from Los Angeles. I had to gauge these subjects' likeliness to be stable even though the latter three had said they had been housed for quite a while. I also weighed the fact that these three women all had problems with their landlords. My gut feeling was they were not very stable in the changing housing market of Los Angeles.

CONCLUDING REMARKS

The spirit, survival skills, and comradery among the former homeless people interviewed leave me optimistic about the human spirit. The distance between the reality of these struggling people and the stereotypes Americans often hold about the homeless is quite phenomenal. Our subjects have overcome obstacles that the middle- or upper-class American probably cannot imagine. Those of us who enter this world must feel as much cognitive dissonance as some of the subjects of the book because these realities defy the "everyday talk" of the culture.

Yet as optimistic as some of these stories make me, unfortunately the realities of life at and near the bottom of American society are such that we must also be pessimistic. We have seen that a number of the subjects may face setbacks. This was most evident in Los Angeles, where several people interviewed mentioned the danger of eviction or displacement looming for them. The housing crisis has been well publicized there, with an increase in development threatening many parts of the city. Increased gentrification was just as present in the Washington, DC; Portsmouth, New Hampshire; Haverhill, Massachusetts; and Portland, Maine areas as well. Income supports are perhaps a little more stable, but there is no guarantee many of the subjects on disability benefits (Social Security disability or SSI) and other benefits will not lose those benefits at some time. Those supported by income or a combination of small income and social benefits are also in danger.

In the educated guess about the future, I was uncertain about only one-sixth of the subjects, but would not be surprised if even one-quarter of the subjects will have to deal with homelessness again. Perhaps these spells will be shorter than previously or perhaps because of the increased sophistication of the subjects and support of others in the community, crises may be averted. But the overall numbers of people and causes of homelessness are not declining and are likely to affect most of our subjects or at least their siblings, children, or friends. In that sense, the small changes that have occurred over the last decades seem extremely inadequate in light of the increased pressure on housing and income and the increased decline of many low-income communities.

APPENDIX I

Finding the Ex-Homeless: Research Methods

There is a long history of qualitative research about poverty[1] and homelessness.[2] The study that informs much of this book is based on interviews with fifty-one formerly homeless people from New England, Southern California, and Washington, DC. Such a study may lack the numbers that can be interviewed by phone or by other means in a large quantitative study; however, at least at the stage where we are in researching this issue, there are also advantages in a smaller study based on personal interviews. Any sort of long-distance contact with this population may be problematic due to the difficulty in locating them, and further, gaining trust from a population that is likely to be quite skeptical of researchers.

There is no way to identify people as "ex-homeless" without some connection to organizations who can identify them. Due to confidentiality, a large study would be difficult because most social service agencies and others in a treatment relationship would not assist in locating them. Moreover, without direct contact with subjects in person, including my interview visits to apartments, it may be difficult to assess the information people give by phone or e-mail or other means. While researchers must accept the veracity of interview subjects, the physical presence in homes of subjects and/or in the milieu where subjects live or participate in activities is considerably helpful. Although this is not an ethnographic study, in many cases, particularly in Portland and Los Angeles, I did have access to other information about the subjects I had met in their natural setting. I used this information with care because I did not feel it appropriate to contradict the interview information and not all of what I overheard or saw would necessarily be true. Subject names, although I had not promised confidentiality, were changed just in case of any problem that might emerge for subjects. In this study, because of its focus, I did not find much sharing of illegal activities or other issues that might compromise people, but in case any material verged on this, I either eliminated it or ensured that the subject was a bit disguised. Subjects received a small monetary stipend to compensate for their time.

As a sociologist and social welfare expert who has written about poor and homeless people, my advantage in doing this research is that I had contacts with a number of ex-homeless people in Portland, Maine, and Los Angeles, California. In Portland, Maine, where I lived for more than two decades, I came to know people both through my research (my book *Checkerboard Square* about Portland's homeless community), and my activism in the community with a variety of groups. Similarly since 2009, I have been going regularly to Southern California, and have been volunteering and assisting the Los Angeles Community Action Network (LACAN), a community organization for the poor based in Skid Row, Los Angeles. The members and activists of LACAN include a lot of ex-homeless people, and their meetings include homeless and ex-homeless people.

Through the kind assistance of some service agencies and advocacy groups, I extended my interviews to Haverhill, Massachusetts, and Portsmouth, New Hampshire, and also interviewed in Washington, DC.[3] Although I cannot suggest that this sample of people is a completely random one, the mix of the five cities provides me a snapshot of some of the demographic variables in homelessness. For example, Los Angeles (one of the "capitals of homelessness," competing with New York City) and Washington, DC, are representative of large urban homelessness in America, and also include a large number of people of color, particularly African Americans. On the other hand, Portland, Portsmouth, and Haverhill are small cities with many people from rural areas coming to these locations because no service is available in their hometowns. Although there are more racial and ethnic minorities among the homeless than the population at large, the numerical majority are white people. The areas also are broad enough that they include urban areas with a good amount of social services and rural, exurban, and suburban areas that lack services.

Except for Washington, DC, my approach was to meet individually at a designated time with the formerly homeless person, sometimes in their own apartments and sometimes at an organization's headquarters (such as LACAN in Los Angeles). Interviewees were asked for biographical and demographic information (age, birthplace, education, etc.), about their time and experiences with homelessness, a description of their current lives, evaluating what helped them leave homelessness, and how they survived financially and emotionally the process of being homeless and now being housed. Most interviews lasted at least an hour and a half. In Portland, Maine, some invaluable help was provided by the Amistad Center, a drop-in center for people with psychiatric histories, who posted signs and encouraged people to meet with me (or my wife Marcia B. Cohen, who was on the Board of Amistad and a professor of social work), by the Preble Street Resource Center, and Homeless Voices for Justice, the former being the largest social service agency for the homeless in Portland, and the latter an advocacy group of formerly homeless people in the area. In addition to two interviews done by Marcia B. Cohen, Angela Desrochers, a longtime former Preble Street worker, assisted by interviewing some people from Preble Street and Florence House, a transitional residence. Gemma Atticks, a graduate student at the University of Southern Maine in Social Work, helped with this book, and also interviewed Peter Driscoll, the executive director of Amistad, for chapter 5. Thanks to the help of two social service agencies, Crossroads, a shelter in Portsmouth, New Hampshire, and Emmaus Inc., a comprehensive service provider in Haverhill, Massachusetts, I was able to contact a number of formerly homeless people in these areas. Interviews were held most often at people's apartments after contacting them by phone or e-mail.

In Los Angeles, three sources of interviewees were found. One was several former students of mine at the California State–Dominguez Hills campus in Carson, California, who had shared with me the fact that they had been homeless. Second, LACAN kindly allowed me to speak at a couple of their meetings and send around sign-up sheets for those who were interested in participating in interviews. Third, the Skid Row theater group LAPD (Los Angeles Poverty Department), which

included quite a few formerly homeless people as actors, was very helpful in facilitating contact with their members and inviting them to be
interviewed. Most interviews in the LA area were conducted at LA-
CAN; it was a convenient place that most of the formerly homeless
people knew.

A difficult task, as may be expected when venturing on a project
such as this, is finding people. Not only do formerly homeless people
usually not announce themselves, but some no longer use social services
or frequent places that have a majority of homeless and poor people. I
was frustrated initially that in Portland, where I had quite a few former
students whom I recalled had been homeless while I was teaching at
the University of Southern Maine, I was unable to reach quite a few of
them. I tried phone numbers I had from the past, the phone book,
Facebook, and so on, but without success. Americans are highly mobile,
and this is particularly true of both young people and poorer people.
Once I was able to find people, I did not have many refusals. One man
who planned to come to LACAN for an interview told me when I called
him that he was reluctant to participate in a study just because he felt
that they did not lead anywhere and could be used in a negative light. I
tried to persuade him, but his mind seemed made up. More commonly,
there were people in all places who were unreachable by phone or e-
mail or did not respond to messages on phone machines or with roommates.

The generous support of the Coalition of the Homeless, the first
national advocacy organization for the homeless dating to 1982 and
based in Washington, DC, allowed me to organize a focus group there
with eight members of their Speakers Bureau, all of whom were now
housed but had been homeless. Members of the focus group were
asked to fill out a short biographical survey, and then joined a discussion
about the issues involved in their homelessness, how they survived, how
they came to be housed, and about their lives generally in the years
since they were homeless.

Altogether, I interviewed fifty-one people, fourteen in Portland,
eight in Haverhill/Portsmouth, twenty-one in the Los Angeles area, and
eight in Washington, DC. Although this is a tip of the iceberg of formerly homeless people, I attempted with general success to make the
sample similar to national figures in terms of gender, family versus
single homelessness, race, and ethnicity. There are clearly areas—edu-

cation, age, employment, etc.—in which the formerly homeless do not resemble the homeless (see the tables below). Having experienced at least two months of being housed (although I sought longer-term formerly homeless people, sometimes the subjects arrived at an interview and stated that they were more recently homeless), my sample ranged in age from their twenties to their sixties, with some people in my study having not been homeless for two decades. This is different from what data we have on shelter homelessness, which tends to be younger (in the twenties and thirties). Additionally (see below), the ex-homeless had more social benefits and a higher level of education than the homeless due both to the aid they got to be housed and the time spent post homelessness to acquire education, training, or new benefits.

One difficulty in the study was the lengthy time needed for interviews with long-term-housed people. I had not anticipated when I started the study that many people would have been housed for seven, fourteen, or even twenty years. With most subjects I had interviewed for other projects as well as this one, I had a strong biographical and chronological focus on the person's life and his or her homelessness. However, when someone was housed for that long, I had to improvise questions to find out more about what they had been doing over such a long period, work-wise, in terms of relationships, and in terms of contacts (if any) with formerly homeless people or service organizations. I would have liked (even after interviews that lasted two or more hours) to have met with each person again to better acquaint myself with the long years some of these subjects were housed. Unfortunately, it was not practical in most cases to do so.

The age difference, combined with some of the likely variables of referral (though not evenly—in Haverhill-Portsmouth I was dependent on agency referral and in DC on members of the Speakers Bureau; Portland and Los Angeles were more variable), such as successful re-entry to housing may make the sample more articulate and "successful" than some other ex-homeless people. In one sense, this is a limitation; however, it should be stressed that the sample has no obvious differences in their length of time homeless, in their use of substances and experience with mental illness, and other variables of homelessness. Yes, these are survivors, but in my experience with a range of ex-homeless people, from former students to clients at social service agencies, there are large numbers of successful survivors.

I see this study as a forerunner for studies that may have more subjects and more locations. I would applaud any effort to interview or otherwise contact a larger sample of formerly homeless. Such an effort would be extremely time consuming and expensive. One strategy might be to take a small number of select cities and focus researchers on the poorer neighborhoods. While no doubt there would be issues—one would miss those who left town and those who, for whatever reason, have moved to nonpoverty areas, and there would always be disputes as to how random one's choices are; it would probably maximize the numbers of people to either go door to door in poor areas or to ascertain through phone numbers a large number of formerly homeless people.

DEMOGRAPHICS OF THIS STUDY

The tables below provide information on our sample, in some cases to compare them with studies of homeless people, but in many cases, since there have been few previous studies completed about the ex-homeless, simply to draw a portrait that was further described in earlier chapters.

Table I.1 may at first look like our sample is high on men and low on families; however, I interviewed only adults. The latest point-in-time homeless data from HUD[4] counts 63.5 percent of the homeless as individuals and 36.5 percent as being in families. However, a great many of the family count consists of children. In the 2015 survey, there were 123,120 children in families; this brings the family number of adults down to 17 percent (73,166 people). Hence adults in families counting for 23 percent is very consistent. The gender count in table I.2 is very close to national figures, where males outnumber females 60 percent to 39.7 percent.

In table I.3 on race,[5] the numbers are nearly exactly what are found for African Americans and whites in most surveys (48.5 percent of homeless people are white, 40.4 percent African American). Latino/Hispanic numbers are lower (nearly 20 percent is found in the HUD study). Native Americans are 2 percent as against 2.7 percent in the HUD study, and my study did not have Pacific Islanders or Asians, both of whose numbers are small in the homeless population. The survey cities except for Los Angeles are low in Latino/Hispanic and Native

Americans, but even in Los Angeles, there is a preponderance of African Americans among the homeless interviewed despite the city's large Latino population.[6]

In table I.4 age is a variable not expected to be the same as currently homeless people. Many homeless people are younger. In my study, where the subject of interest is the formerly homeless, I interviewed people who had been homeless nearly a generation ago as well as just a few years ago. Hence my sample is far older. In table I.5 (length of time housed) this statistic is not for comparison; rather I felt that this was important because housing the homeless is not always successful over the long term for a number of reasons. The group interviewed here was primarily long-term housed.

In table I.6, the number of people working full-time appears fairly consistent with other studies. Some studies quote large numbers working and if one adds the "some work" to full-time, the majority is working. However, many positions pay far too little to support a person, and are being held in combination with benefits, in particular Social Security Disability and Supplemental Security Income or SSI (more than half the sample), or veterans' pensions or Social Security retirement (OAS-DI). As was discussed in the text, the cost of housing in the areas studied was far too great to be affordable on most benefits (with disability or retirement being best), and the possibility of highly paid work is low except for some exceptional people who had previous high-level job skills. There was a small number of people on other benefits such as TANF (formerly AFDC) or general assistance, a program not available in many states, but that is available in California and Maine, for example.

Table I.7 shows the education status of the sample. There has been far less study of this data than of gender, race, or even work status of homeless people. Again, although because this table includes people who went on with their education after their homelessness, the sample is probably a bit higher in education than a homeless sample. Still, nearly half have only a high school diploma or less and the nearly one-fifth who have had some college (including some with just a few courses) do not have good prospects in the employment market unless they finished college.

Table I.8 explores the social class status of the families of origin of those interviewed. This is an area that has hardly been studied, but is of interest because some people exaggerate homelessness as "it can happen to anyone." Although this is technically true, and there are some individuals from higher classes, generally the findings (about 65 percent) are from poor or working-class families, which fits my experience with asking people who are homeless what their socioeconomic background is. I used classic sociology to place blue-collar or service workers in the working class, and those with low incomes, unstable work, or on benefits as poor. The break between middle and upper class is a difficult one. Most middle-class people were professionals, small-business owners, or mid-level executives. I coded as upper-middle only those who had higher positions or had come into enough income to have high levels of consumption and status.

I produce table I.9 with caution, for while some interviewees noted alcohol, drugs, or mental illness as causes of homelessness, others described these as an intervening variable or a state that occurred when they were homeless, not before. Still, it is important in terms of the great progress many of these people have made, that the vast majority did have to wrestle with addiction or a mental disorder or both. Although statistics about homeless people's substance use and mental disorder are contested, many experts put them at least at 30 percent each.

Table I.10 shows the current housing status of the sample. "Regular" apartment is used to distinguish from others below. It is simply a unit in an apartment building or house that is rented. Elderly/disabled housing is usually federally funded housing run by a nonprofit or government program in which occupants must be seniors or disabled (in terms of government disability programs). These often have long waiting lists. I use the *transitional/supportive* term for any nonprofit housing specifically for former homeless people or in some cases related populations. Some of these units are meant to be short-term (hence the term *transitional*), however, even these vary in whether they actually force people out. Most of these units claim to be *supportive* by providing services on site or by contract—for example mental health and substance use counseling. SRO hotels are single room occupancies, which are usually quite small, privately owned, and often lacking in even kitchen and bathroom facilities that residents must share. *Public housing* here means only public housing projects, not Section 8 vouchers (many of those in "regular apartments" are assisted by Section 8). *Boarding house* was once a very common type of housing for low-income and working people; they are like dormitories or have small rooms and are usually privately owned; unlike transitional residences, they usually lack support services.

In my experience talking to the homeless and formerly homeless, other than public housing or owning a home, the list is somewhat in preferential order. Those who got into senior housing usually were relatively free of stigma and in better conditions. This was true, although to a lesser extent, with some of the transitional/supportive residences. Although not universal, many people interviewed complained about SRO and boarding homes. I did not interview enough people in (or formerly in) public housing to comment here.

Table I.I. Category of Homeless

Category	Sample number	Percentage of total
Single Male	30	58.8
Single female	8	15.7
Family	13	25.5

Table I.2. Gender

Category	Sample number	Percentage of total
Male	32	61.5
Female	20	38.5

Note: The total number is one higher than the sample; a male/female couple interviewed together.

Table I.3. Race and Ethnicity among Sample

Category	Sample number	Percentage of total
White	21	41.2
Latino	5	9.8
African American	24	47.0
Native American	1	2.0

Table I.4. Age of Those Interviewed

Category	Sample number	Percentage of total
60s	10	19.6
50s	21	41.2
40s	10	19.6
30s	8	15.7
20s	2	3.9

Table I.5. Length of Time Housed

Category	Sample number	Percentage of total
Long-term (over two years)	35	68.6
Short-term (less than two years)	16	31.4

Table I.6. Source of Income/Work

Category	Sample number	Percentage of total
Primarily benefits: disability, retirement, and veterans' pensions	34	66.6
Full time work	9	17.6
Some work	24	47.1

Note: Numbers are above 100% because a number of subjects combined some work and benefits.

Table I.7. Education

Category	Sample number	Percentage of total
BA or more	11	22.9 (4 with MA or more)
Associate's degree	3	6.3
AA student	1	2.1
Some college	10	20.8
High school graduate	10	20.8
GED	1	2.1
Less than high school	12	25
Unknown	3	5.9

Table I.8. Socioeconomic Class of Origin

Category	Sample number	Percentage of total
Upper-middle class	2	3.9
Middle class/professional	9	17.6
Farmer	1	2.0
Middle/working class	5	9.8
Skilled working class	20	39.2
Poor	12	23.5
Unknown	2	3.9

Table I.9. Alcoholism, Drugs, and Mental Illness (Self-Described) in Sample

Category	Sample number	Percentage of total
Alcohol/drugs	26	51.0
Mental Illness	27	52.9
Both (i.e., dual diagnoses)[a]	11	21.6
None (or Unknown)	9	17.6

Note: Numbers are above 100 percent; 42 people cited at least one or the other (mental illness or alcohol or drugs) and nine none.
[a]Several former homeless people had concluded that substance use was a form of "self-medicating" their psychological issues, and in some cases their state of homelessness. Professionals now recognize the "dual diagnosis" of substance use and mental illness, although I am not certain I would describe all of the subjects this way. Some people used substances while homeless, but not later, and some came to believe that they were mentally ill after being homeless.

Table I.10. Type of Current Housing

Category	Sample number	Percentage of total
Regular apartment	34	66.6
Elderly/disabled housing	6	11.8
Transitional/supportive housing	4	7.8
SRO hotels	4	7.8
Own house	1	2.0
Public housing	1	2.0
Boarding house	1	2.0

APPENDIX II

The Ex-Homeless in History and among Celebrities

Despite the stigma of homelessness, there has been a surprising fascination with aspects of homelessness, its culture, and conditions. It is important to remind ourselves that a great deal of the late nineteenth- and early twentieth-century American culture involved the tramp, hobo, and vagrant. There was always another side to the hostility of the law and the upper classes to the tramp and the homeless. Ordinary working people sympathized with the poor, and while some towns hunted down vagrants, some people affixed symbols to their houses, indicating that they would give alms and sustenance. Both Margaret Sanger, the birth control advocate, and Elizabeth Gurley Flynn, the radical organizer, remember their fathers taking in tramps and wanderers as a matter of course.[1] With the polarization of the Great Railroad Strike of 1877, the Haymarket Affair of 1886, the Pullman Strike of 1893, and other incidents, not a few people (particularly foreign immigrants, the new stigmatized poor) sympathized with the "dangerous classes."

By the 1905–1917 period, some of the more radical years in American history, the formation of the radical "Wobblies" (the International Workers of the World—IWW), which drew members from the ranks of migrant workers, glorified the road and the tramp, famously singing Joe Hill's song "Hallelujah! I'm a Bum." Activism among migrant workers in the West and among mill workers in the East were held together by a variety of socialist and anarchist ideologies and a solidarity for low-paid workers. Although the Wobblies never had more than 100,000 members, they and the Socialist Party of Eugene V. Debs (which drew a fair percentage of votes between 1900 and 1916) had a broad influence among working people and the poor.

A great deal of our culture in fact was built on takeoffs of old populist and Wobbly ways. *The Wizard of Oz* is based on a children's story by Frank L. Baum and was an allegory to a populist future in which the farmer and worker would run things. The song "Big Rock Candy Mountain," later made popular by folk singer Burl Ives, was based on a Wobbly song where hoboes run free, don't have to work, drink whenever they want, and lead a heavenly existence. The phrase "Coxey's Army" was based on an 1893 march of men throughout the nation to Washington, DC, led by General Jacob Coxey, calling for jobs for the unemployed. "Mulligan Stew" and other makeshift brews came from hobo camps where any food people could scrounge were placed in a large tin. Jack London, one of the first well-known people born from a poor family, started "tramping" with a branch of Coxey's Army.

TWO FAMOUS FORMERLY HOMELESS PEOPLE WHO MADE GOOD—JACK LONDON AND CHARLIE CHAPLIN

One way to look at how poverty and homelessness in America has a flip side of fascination, interest, and appeal is through the lives of people who came from a poor background and became famous in America. Both the author and activist Jack London (1876–1916) and the transplanted Englishman Charlie Chaplin (1889–1977), who invented the popular character of the "tramp," had a big impact on America.

Biographer Alex Kershaw describes writer Jack London "as doing more to increase class consciousness than any other writer of his time";[2] he might have added writer Theodore Dreiser, whose fame was contemporaneous with London. London grew up in Oakland, California, as the illegitimate child of a downwardly mobile mother (typhoid fever had laid her low and left her scarred and psychologically bereft). London was seen as his mother's "badge of shame" and was treated harshly. Like many Americans, he experienced child labor, having to work at a young age at a cannery for many hours a day. London later fell in with local gangs and became a "brawler" and heavy drinker. Originally hired to patrol the coast against pirates in the Oakland harbor, he switched sides and joined "a group of young hoboes" who were themselves pirates.[3] Afterward, he took "to riding the rails" as millions of young men did between the Civil War and the Great Depression and joined "Kelly's Army," a branch of Coxey's Army.[4] While tramping, London was arrested for vagrancy in Niagara Falls, New York, and was clubbed on the head and then forced to spend thirty days in the penitentiary. This experience helped to radicalize London.

London became a speaker at the public soapbox in Oakland and was called the "boy socialist." He even ran for mayor of the city unsuccessfully. When London achieved literary success as he did in the early twentieth century it was mostly with his masculine youth stories such as *Call of the Wild* and *White Fang*, but he also wrote nonfiction and political books. Older people knew that London was an IWW supporter and a socialist, although he later would fall out with these organizations. Biographer James Haley notes that London's radicalization through his experience with tramps was profound; London said they "held a deep wisdom."

> Among the hoboes, however, he found men who were able to compensate for their banishment from the economy with a vivid life of the mind. They lived on handouts, but they understood life in a way he did not. Their experience presented him with a profound and alluring mystery.[5]

Not all of London's appeal to readers, by any means, was his politics or social class, but it is interesting that one of the first poor people to become famous in America had been a tramp and saw himself on the side of the tramps and hoboes.

Born in London in 1887 to two English vaudeville personalities, Charlie Chaplin not only endured a Dickensian childhood with repeated losses but went on to perfect the image of the "tramp" as the comedic and tragic symbol, in many ways a magnificent contribution of social class to public imagery.

Even many years later when working on his autobiography, Chaplin realized how deep were the blows and the losses he had suffered: "The rich and famous and fulfilled man whom the world sees still considers himself a victim maimed for life by the early catastrophic shock."[6] Chaplin and his brother Sidney would lose both parents—their father through drink and separation from their mother, and their mother to poverty, and then mental illness. Chaplin was only one year old when his father left them and went to live with another woman. Although Hannah, Chaplin's mother, went to the law courts to sue her husband, the case did not go well for her and she did not receive adequate support.

When Chaplin was six years old, along with his mother and his brother Sidney he entered the Lambert Borough workhouse. Chaplin wrote of the boys having to separate from their mother and "the shock of seeing Mother enter the visiting room garbed in workhouse clothes."[7] But things would get worse as the boys were sent to the Hanwell School for Orphans and Destitute Children, twelve miles from London, and further separated from each other as they were placed in different grades. Chaplin recalled,

> It was a forlorn existence. Sadness was in the air. . . . How I disliked those walks [through the village where] the locals [were] staring at us! We were known as inmates of the "booby hatch," a slang term for the workhouse. [The punishment of offenses] took place every Friday . . . and boys . . . marched in and lined up in military fashion [to see the disciplining of boys by canes.] The spectacle was terrifying. I remembered witnessing my first flogging [and] . . . my heart thumping.[8]

Both shame and stigma were well known to Chaplin as a boy. In his autobiography, Chaplin revises Sigmund Freud as to what factors in life are most important: "Unlike Freud, I do not believe sex is the most important element in the complexity of behavior. Cold, hunger, and the shame of poverty are more likely to affect one's psychology."[9]

In a similar vein, he recalls:

> I was well aware of the social stigma of our poverty. Even the poorest children sat down to a home-cooked Sunday dinner. A roast at home meant respectability, a ritual that distinguished one poor class from another. Those who could not sit down to Sunday dinner at home were of the mendicant class, and we were that.[10]

In English vaudeville, actors were well aware of the characters of tramps and inebriates. English music halls were primarily working-class entertainment, and the people laughed heartily at the stock figures. What Chaplin was able to do was popularize the tramp as an anti-authority figure who gained huge sympathy of twenty-five years of movie-goers.

Chaplin's very creation of his alter ego, the tramp, was a tremendously creative way to introduce a class icon with whom the vast majority of people at the time could identify. Chaplin discusses how the pursuit of the tramp by higher-class figures with whom he interferes is part of the joy of his films:

> The delight that the average person takes in seeing wealth and luxuries in trouble. . . people get a satisfaction from seeing the rich get the worst of things. The reason, of course, lies in the fact that nine-tenths of the people in the world are poor, and secretly resent the wealth of the other tenth. [11]

The class-based humor of the films did not escape everyone's attention, and just as there was opposition in many quarters to the rise of film as a medium generally in the first decades of the twentieth century, some protested Chaplin's films in particular. A speaker at the Women's Alliance at a Unitarian Church in Brooklyn called him "a moral menace. His is a low type of humor that appeals only to the lowest type of intellect. I cannot understand how any resident of Flatbush can go see [his films]." [12]

This does not presume by any means that the tramp was *only* a lower-class street figure. The empathy people felt for him came greatly from his malleability. As Chaplin describes the early invention of the tramp in his career, he notes, "You know this fellow is many-sided, a tramp, a gentleman, a poet, a dreamer, a lonely fellow, always hopeful of romance and adventure. He would have you believe he is a scientist, a musician, a duke, a polo-player." Yet he adds quickly in his autobiography, "However, he is not above picking up cigarette-butts or robbing a baby of its candy. And of course, if the occasion warrants, he will kick a lady in the rear—but only in extreme anger." It seems as if primarily his heart was most in the tramp as a lovable everyman who was out of place in society: as his first demonstration of the tramp, he "[found himself] in the hotel lobby [and] I felt I was an imposter posing as one of the guests, but in reality I was a tramp just wanting a little shelter. I entered and stumbled over the foot of a lady. I turned and raised my hat apologetically, then turned and raised my hat to the cuspidor."[13] The funny, stumbling figure, taken along with most of Chaplin's autobiography, shows how the tramp mirrored Chaplin's discomfort with all forms of higher society.

Steven Ross calls Chaplin "the first political movie star" in that he

> was at the vanguard of a new form of political communication that bypassed traditional authority figures and spoke directly to millions of immigrants and working-class people who felt as though no one cared about them . . . [while] his silent films did not promote communism . . . they did mock the power and legitimacy of those who gave ordinary Americans a hard time; employers, foremen, police, judges, the idle rich, and even world leaders.[14]

Chaplin's anti-authoritarian tramp hit the United States in 1914 and within one year made him a millionaire. Already in 1914, his name was so well known that *The Knockout* was advertised as a "Charlie Chaplin film."[15] In 1915 there was, as David Robinson puts it, "the great Chaplin explosion": "every newspaper carried cartoons and poems about him. He became a character in cartoon strips. . . . there were Chaplin dolls, toys, books. . . . Ida Lupino sang 'that Charlie Chaplin Walk.'"[16]

OTHER FAMOUS HOMELESS FIGURES AND "RIDING THE RAILS"

Although few poor people become famous, much less achieve the fame London and Chaplin did, there are other famous Americans who were homeless. This group includes those placed in institutions such as poorhouses or poor farms and also at orphanages, an experience far more common to children in the past than it is today. Sometimes the parents of these children were homeless, but sometimes they just could not afford to maintain children on their small resources.

The "miracle worker" Anne Sullivan (1866–1936), so famous for her teaching of Helen Keller, was, like Chaplin, one of the more famous people to come out of the poorhouse experience. She grew up in dire poverty in a town in western Massachusetts with her father, who was an alcoholic, and her mother who had tuberculosis, struggling to raise a family. After her mother died, her father, caught in the great depression of 1873 and his own problems, sent Anne and her brother Jimmy to the Massachusetts State Almshouse in Tewksbury, where Anne ended up as an "inmate" for four and half years, her brother dying shortly after entering the poorhouse of a tubercular hip. Sullivan herself was "half-blind," plagued by a disease called trachoma that is treatable today. Sullivan luckily was found at the almshouse in 1880 by a Massachusetts official who got her transferred to the Perkins School for the Blind, where she graduated as valedictorian in 1886. A year later the director of Perkins sent her to help a young blind deaf-mute in Alabama named Helen Keller. Sullivan would become one of the most famous Americans of the time and still is one of the most famous women.[17]

Though there are likely far more (the names of poorhouses kept changing because of their stigma to almshouses, workhouses, city farms, county farms, poor farms, city homes, county homes, etc.) two other famous people who spent time in these facilities was the reporter Henry Stanley (1841–1904), most famous for his finding Dr. Livingstone in Africa, who spent time in a British workhouse as a youth, and the American sharpshooter Annie Oakley (1860–1926), who was also an inmate and later a "bound out" child (an early form of foster care used for poor children) with another family by the institution (ANB, 2010).[18]

Perhaps the most famous of the many Americans who grew up in orphanages or institutions for children was legendary baseball star Babe Ruth (1895–1948). Called the "Babe" in fact because many of his first fellow ball players believed he was left as a foundling at an institution, Ruth did live for a while with his German immigrant family, who struggled with him from a young age. He began as a young child to wander the streets, steal, and get into other mischief. He was committed at age seven to an Industrial School (a combination orphanage, reformatory, and juvenile home) in Baltimore. Ruth fared well at the school, though he was rather unsocialized to the outside world when he became a baseball player, and evidently needed help with the rudiments of life in the outside world.[19]

Other famous people who spent time in orphanages included singers Ella Fitzgerald (1917–1996) and Billie Holiday (1915–1959); actor Steve McQueen (1930–1980), who went to a juvenile home; actress Marilyn Monroe (1926–1962), who spent time in an orphanage; author Harold Robbins (1916–1977); writer William Saroyan (1908–1981), baseball player and later minister Billy Sunday (1862–1935); and writer Richard Wright (1908–1960).

Not surprisingly, there are some famous people who were physically (or as today's experts call it "literally") homeless as well as housed by a variety of institutions such as poorhouses and orphanages. An interesting distinction that is rarely discussed is that between children and adults forced into the streets and the more than a few famous Americans (almost all male) who took to "riding the rails" or "tramping" on their own. The distinction is not always as large as it might seem. Few of the latter people had any wealth, and most identified with the "road" either artistically, culturally, or politically, but there may have been some degree of voluntariness about it.

Some examples of famous Americans who seem to have been homeless due to economic reasons include the famous dancer and choreographer Alvin Ailey (1930–1989), who grew up dirt poor and lived with his mother as they crossed Texas looking for work and without a home in the 1930s; singer Ella Fitzgerald (1917–1996), who as a child ran away from an orphanage and was homeless for some time in New York City; John Garfield (1913–1952), the famous tough-guy actor of the 1930s–1940s, who was homeless as a child after his mother died and his father abandoned him; jazz-blues star Billie Holiday (1915–1959), who spent a lot of her childhood and teen years on the streets in both Baltimore and New York City; Steve McQueen (1930–1980), the future film star, also was a homeless teenager wandering Los Angeles; film star and sex icon Marilyn Monroe (1926–1962), who spent some time homeless before making it in Hollywood, both on the streets and what we would call "couch surfing"; and feminist leader and political candidate Victoria Woodhull (1838–1927), who was homeless with her children in the 1870s.[20]

By following words like "hobo" and "hoboing" or "tramp" or "tramping" in sources such as the American Biography Online, one can find other people who made a practice of wandering. Poets Vachel Lindsay (1879–1931) and Carl Sandburg (1878–1967) proudly lived in the first decades of the twentieth century going from city to town and writing, doing some work to support themselves, and "slept rough" or sometimes gained a bed for the night. Famous heavyweight boxing champion to be Jack Johnson (1876–1946) spent many of his early years going from city to city finding boxing matches and even exploitative tournaments to fight in. No one seems to have been surprised that he was "tramping." Another boxing champion to be homeless was Jack Dempsey (1895–1983). He was born poor, as was Johnson, and left home to hobo from 1911 to 1916, when he found some success in the ring. Author James Michener (1907–1997), also born in poverty, left his adopted family and traveled for years in the 1920s through most of the United States.[21]

The largest number of American males "rode the rails" during the Great Depression, when the combination of massive nationwide economic depression and the continued availability of outdoor and temporary work around parts of the western United States made this a frequent haunt for many people. Among the famous there was Nelson Algernon (1908–1981), the famous writer; Robert Mitchum (1917–1997), later the famous actor (Mitchum was supposedly arrested for vagrancy in Savannah, Georgia, and served on a chain gang, but some dispute this); and painter Jackson Pollock (1912–1956). Melvin Belli (1907–1996), later a famous lawyer, though from a prosperous family, decided to ride the rails for six months in the Depression as part of witnessing poverty in America.[22]

The experience of "riding the rails" remains alive in many parts of America based on many stories I have heard from self-described "travelers," "homeless," and "street people" today. America is, after all, the nation of wanderlust, of geographical mobility, of "Go West, Young Man," and of road movies. The tradition has, of course, become more obscure to most affluent or middle-class Americans, but there is something about the trip across America that has stirred the fascination, if not actual wandering. The "road," more than bringing the possibility of better jobs and pay or at least enough to get by, realizes the possibility of relieving the home family of "one more mouth to feed," particularly a hungry adult male. This may be why my father always mentioned to me "riding the rails," although I don't think his family was quite dirt-poor in the depression. Moreover, on the road, one tests one's mettle, strength, and abilities, and finds one's place in society. The fellow travelers are seen as allies and buddies while railroad "bulls" and other authorities are part of the narrative of repression and violence.

CURRENT CELEBRITIES WHO WERE HOMELESS

But it is not just old traditions that cause me to suggest there is ambivalence about the homeless that includes some identification with their plight. A recent cultural tendency can be seen in a surprising number of news sources and websites covering a story about "Celebrities Who Have Been Homeless" in the last two years (including ABC News, CNN, Huffington Post, KCRA-TV, and many others). It was not clear how this story arose, but a variety of sources trumpeted between eighteen and as many as twenty-six stars who they said had been homeless. The qualification for such listing seems loose of course, and most slept in a car or van, usually at the beginning of their acting career. Some stars had only a very short period of "homelessness." Still, it is interesting that these stars themselves and the media outlets saw this as a rather attractive story.

Some people will hasten to add, with some support, that these stories serve to buttress the status quo by showing homelessness or poverty as ills that can be overcome by good luck and talent, and hence the star treatment certainly takes no political or socioeconomic analysis as necessary to its story. But while the mass media will, of course, not take on the "American Dream," it is interesting when something as astounding only a number of decades ago (homelessness) draws such everyday comment, and now a state (homelessness) that is accepted in the media as being rather common. It does support two thoughts: homelessness is far more common than many believe, and some people do rise to do well in society.

It is difficult to tell how much truth there is in these stories. I was able to verify about six stories as involving these stars: movie star Halle Berry had lived in a homeless shelter in New York City in 1989 (though her background was not poor and she had a community college degree); Shania Twain, the Canadian singer-songwriter, did grow up very poor, and at one point her mother drove the family four hundred miles to a homeless shelter in Toronto; rapper-singer-songwriter Lil' Kim did grow up in a poor neighborhood in Brooklyn, and for unclear reasons was thrown out of the house either by her father or brother (there are different accounts) and lived on the streets for at least a while; actress Hillary Swank did live out of a car with her mother, but just until they got enough money to rent in California; actor Jim Carrey was born poor in Canada—his father was a janitor and the family lived out of a van for a while; and actor Sylvester Stallone, also from a poor family, was homeless for a short time in New York City before he got work, and slept in the New York City Port Authority Bus Station.[23]

Others for whom I was unable to verify information and/or their socioeconomic backgrounds include comedian Drew Carey, singer Kelly Clarkson, musician Kurt Cobain, actor Daniel Craig, actress Carmen Electra, actor Kelsey Grammer, comedian-entertainer Steve Harvey, radio personality Donald Imus, singer-songwriter Jewel, billionaire Steve Jobs, TV personality David Letterman, singer-actress Jennifer Lopez, TV personality Dr. Phil McGraw, singer Jim Morrison, business consultant and author Suze Orman, actor Martin Sheen, actor William Shatner, and movie director Tyler Perry. No doubt some couch surfed or lived in cars, but for how long they were homeless is not clear.

In addition, care must be taken to clarify which time period is involved. While the economic satisfaction of the postwar period has been clearly overstated, it is probably true that today's celebrity stories reflect the harder economic times of the 1970s onward rather than the 1945–1965 period. Only by securing complete biographical facts and comparing the exact years and places involved can we get a real sense of any representativeness of the celebrity homelessness.

But again what is most interesting to me is not exactly how many stars to consider "homeless" or "almost homeless," but this new competition for being not only "one of the people" but having come from the very bottom. Generally these types of competition are more common in periods like the Great Depression, when times are so bad; people have to strive to identify with higher-class entertainers. That this is occurring now is interesting, perhaps mirroring our own poor economic times, even though in some ways, economic indicators are well above several years ago. It almost seems as if it is "in" to be poor (once again).

Although the numbers may not be huge, the large number of examples of people who were homeless in our history and apparently celebrities who were homeless before their stardom does show that the stigma of homelessness and continual dismissal of people who were homeless is simply without merit and a matter of class prejudice.

NOTES

1. GIVING VOICE TO THE EX-HOMELESS

1. US Department of Housing and Urban Development (HUD), *The 2014 Annual Assessment Report on the Homeless*, https://www.hudexchange.info/resources/documents/2014-AHAR-Part1.pdf.

2. B. Link, E. Susser, A. Streve, J. Phelan, R. Moore, and E. Struening, "Lifetime Prevalence of Homelessness in the United States," *American Journal of Public Health* 84, no. 12 (December 1994): 1907–12; J. Phelan and B. Link, "Who Are "the Homeless"? Reconsidering the Stability and Composition of the Homeless Population," *American Journal of Public Health* 89, no. 9 (September 1999): 1334–38; and P. A. Toro et al., "Homelessness in Europe and the United States: A Comparison of Prevalence and Public Opinion," *Journal of Social Issues* 63, no. 3 (2007): 505–24.

3. See E. J. Goetz, *New Deal Ruins: Race, Economic Justice, and Public Housing Policy* (Ithaca, NY: Cornell University Press, 2013) for a good account of the current privatization of public housing.

4. Historically, there has always been a struggle as to what to call people without homes. In the nineteenth and well into the twentieth centuries, labels such as "tramp," "hobo," or "vagabond" were used. In the 1930s, under the New Deal, a more neutral label of "transient" was used. But in the early years of the most modern period of homelessness, advocacy groups such as the Coalition for the Homeless waged a struggle with the *New York Times* over replacing vagabond and vagrant with "homeless," which they won. See D. Wagner, *Confronting Homelessness: Poverty, Politics, and the Failure of Social Policy* (Boulder, CO: Lynne Rienner, 2012), chapters 3–4. Unfortunately, the

"homeless" label, while better than earlier ones, does not seem to have reduced the stigma of homeless people.

5. Discussions with homeless people in "North City"—see D. Wagner, *Checkerboard Square: Culture and Resistance in a Homeless Community* (Boulder, CO: Westview, 1993), 33—as well as my experiences with homeless people in Los Angeles indicate that relatively few panhandle, and in some homeless circles, a stigma attaches to it.

6. C. Hoch and R. Slayton, *New Homeless and Old* (Philadelphia: Temple University Press, 1989).

7. *Tent City, U.S.A.* (New York: Oprah Winfrey Network, 2012).

8. M. Wakin, *Otherwise Homeless: Vehicle Living and the Culture of Homelessness* (Boulder, CO: First Forum, 2013).

9. J. Wasserman and J. Clair, *At Home on the Street: People, Poverty and the Hidden Culture of Homelessness* (Boulder, CO: Lynne Rienner, 2009).

10. For discussion see J. Blau, *The Visible Poor: Homelessness in the United States* (New York: Oxford University Press, 1992); C. Bogard, *Seasons Such as These: How Homelessness Took Shape in America* (New York: Aldine De Gruyter, 2003); and K. Hopper, *Reckoning with Homelessness* (Ithaca, NY: Cornell University Press, 2001).

11. P. Rossi, *Down and Out in America: The Origins of Homelessness* (Chicago: University of Chicago Press, 1989).

12. *New York Times*, "Ending Chronic Homelessness," editorial, March 13, 2002, A24.

13. National Coalition for the Homeless, *Safety Network*, 1983–2014.

14. T. Pippert, *Road Dogs and Loners: Family Relationships among Homeless Men*. Lanham, MD: Lexington, 2007.

15. For one of the earlier descriptions, see B. Bluestone and B. Harrison, *The Deindustrialization of America* (New York: Basic, 1982).

16. Goetz, *New Deal Ruins*.

17. S. Hays, *Flat Broke with Children: Women in the Age of Welfare Reform* (Oxford, UK: Oxford University Press, 2003).

18. A. Benavie, *Drugs: America's Holy War* (New York: Routledge, 2009); and M. Alexander, *The New Jim Crow: Mass Incarceration in the Age of Colorblindness* (New York: New Press, 2012).

19. See, for example, D. Wagner, *The New Temperance: The American Obsession with Sin and Vice* (Boulder, CO: Westview-Harper Collins, 1997) and C. Rainerman and H. Levine, eds., *Crack in America: Demon Drugs and Social Justice* (Berkeley: University of California Press, 1997).

20. D. Wagner and P. White, "Breaking the Silence: Homelessness and Race," in *Routledge Handbook on Poverty in the United States*, ed. S. Haymes, M. Vidal de Haymes, and R. Miller (New York: Routledge, 2013).

21. See graphs on the coverage of the issue in United States broadcast media and some newspapers in Wagner, *Confronting Homelessness*.

22. S. Roberts, "Reagan on Homelessness: Many Choose to Live in the Streets," *New York Times*, December 23, 1988, 1.

23. Wagner, *Confronting Homelessness*, chapter 2.

24. *Outriders* (New York: Skylight Films, 2003); *Living Broke in Boom Times* (New York: Skylight Films, 2007).

25. National Economic and Social Rights Initiative, *More Than a Roof*, video (2010).

26. A. Horwitz, *Creating Mental Illness* (Chicago: University of Chicago Press, 2002).

27. Wagner, *Confronting Homelessness*; Wagner, *The New Temperance*.

28. See A. Gewirtz, D. S. DeGarmo, S. Lee, N. Morrell, and G. August, "Two-Year Outcomes of Early Risers Prevention Trial with Formerly Homeless Families Residing in Supportive Housing," *Journal of Family Psychology* 29, no. 2 (April 2015): 242–52; R. Hawkins and C. Abrams, "Disappearing Acts: The Social Networks of Formerly Homeless Individuals with Co-Occurring Disorders," *Social Science and Medicine* 65, no. 10 (2007): 2031–42; S. Kidd, J. Karabanow, J. Hughes, and F. Tyler, "Brief Report: Youth Pathways out of Homelessness—Preliminary Findings," *Journal of Adolescence* 36, no. 6 (December 2013): 1035–37; D. K. Padgett, B. T. Smith, B. F. Henwood, and E. Tiderington, "Life Course Adversity in the Lives of Formerly Homeless Persons with Serious Mental Illness: Context and Meaning," *American Journal of Orthopsychiatry* 82, no. 3 (July 2012): 421–30; M. Patterson, A. Moniruzzaman, and J. Somers, "Community Participation and Belonging among Formerly Homeless Adults with Mental Illness after 12 Months of Housing First in Vancouver, British Columbia: A Randomized Controlled Trial," *Community Mental Health Journal* 50, no. 5 (2014): 604–11; A. Patterson and R. Tweed, "Escaping Homelessness: Anticipated and Perceived Facilitators," *Journal of Community Psychology* 37, no. 7 (2009): 846–58; E. Raphael-Greenfield and S. Gutman, "Understanding the Lived Experienced of Formerly Homeless Adults as They Transition to Supportive Housing," *Occupational Therapy in Mental Health* 31, no. 1 (January–March 2015): 35–49; and J. Tsai, A. Klee, J. Remmele, and L. Harkness, "Life after Supported Housing: A Case Series of Formerly Homeless Clients in the Department of Veterans Affairs-Supportive Housing Program 20 Years Later," *Journal of Community Psychology* 41, no. 8 (November 2013): 1039–46.

29. M. Shinn et al., "Predictors of Homelessness among Families in New York City: From Shelter Request to Housing Stability," *American Journal of Public Health* 88, no. 11 (November 1998): 1651–57.

30. A. Semuels, "The Best Way to End Homelessness," *The Atlantic*, July 11, 2015, accessed August 15, 2016, https://www.theatlantic.com/business/archive/2015/07/the-best-way-to-end-homelessness/398282.

31. I have also studied patterns of utilization of a large number of poorhouses, also called poor farms or county or city homes, from the 1870s to as late as the 1960s. These "houses" were extremely similar, if not identical to homeless shelters, and their total annual admissions were many multiples of their available beds at any time. Although some "inmates" as they were called might be elderly or disabled, among those who were not there was a great turnover in attendance for multiple reasons including the cold weather of winter, and then the arrival of warmer seasons.

32. Wagner, *Checkerboard Square*, 33.

2. PROFILES OF FORMERLY HOMELESS PEOPLE

1. A big problem in the social services, and perhaps in social science inquiry, is a lack of consensus on what measures should be signs of a person's progress. Although a good thing in the sense that one cultural or national set of norms is now taken as suspect, on the other hand, it makes for a certain confusion in what the millions of people in human services mean by what they are doing. If they resist the pure governmental and normative demands—get people off the street, make them work and stop abusing substances—then one runs the danger of sounding existential. However, in some way or another many helpers from nonprofessionals to social workers or clergy do recognize that community reentry and recovery from trauma is an important emotional event in people's lives even if they do not have a middle-class lifestyle.

2. I have never seen any literature on this, but for some people there does seem to be a ladder of housing on which they stumble down the rungs before becoming totally homeless. Beyond the cumulative loss of money, family, friends, and coworkers who might have served as checks on behavior may be gradually shed as a person (such as in Bob's case) moves further into some psychological or physical deterioration.

3. E. H. Erikson, *Identity and the Life Cycle* (New York: Norton, 1980).

4. R. Xia, "One in Ten California State Students Are Homeless, Study Says," *Los Angeles Times*, June 20, 2016, accessed December 24, 2016, http://www.latimes.com/local/lanow/la-me-cal-state-homelessness-20160620-snap-story.html.

5. P. Zonkel, "CSU Report: 10% of Students Experience Homelessness," *Long Beach Press Telegram*, February 27, 2016.

6. D. Wagner, *Checkerboard Square: Culture and Resistance in a Homeless Community* (Boulder, CO: Westview, 1993).

7. *The Soloist* (Los Angeles: Dreamworks, 2009).

8. *Lost Angels: Skid Row Is My Home* (Los Angeles: Cinema Libre Studio, 2013).

9. M. Rosario, E. W. Scrimshaw, and J. Hunter, "Risk Factors for Homelessness among Lesbian, Gay, and Bisexual Youths: A Developmental Milestone Approach," *Children and Youth Services Review* 34, no. 1 (2012): 186–93; and J. M. Van Leeuwen, S. Boyle, S. Salomonsen-Sautel, D. N. Baker, J. T. Garcia, A. Hoffman, and C. J. Hopfer, "Lesbian, Gay, and Bisexual Homeless Youth: An Eight-City Public Health Perspective," *Child Welfare* 85, no. 2 (2006): 151–70.

10. C. Bawden, "Homelessness and Domestic Violence," *Parity* 22, no. 10 (2009): 1032–47; E. Malosi and G. Hague, "Women, Housing, Homelessness, and Domestic Violence," *Women's Studies International Forum* 20, no. 3 (May–June 1997): 397–409.

3. THE FIGHT TO SECURE AND STAY IN HOUSING

1. B. Weissman and G. Leiner, *Home: The Langston Terrace Dwellings* (Washington, DC: Columbia Historical Society, 1991).

2. N. D. Bloom and F. Umbach, *Public Housing Myths: Perception, Reality, and Social Policy* (Ithaca, NY: Cornell University Press, 2015); and E. J. Goetz, *New Deal Ruins: Race, Economic Justice, and Public Housing Policy* (Ithaca, NY: Cornell University Press, 2013).

3. Goetz, *New Deal Ruins*.

4. J. Eligon, "An Indelible Black-and-White Line," *New York Times*, August 8, 2015.

5. M. Byrne, "Hundreds of Mainers Line Up for Housing Assistance," *Portland Press Herald*, April 10, 2013, 1.

6. M. Lipsky, *Street Level Bureaucracy* (New York: Russell Sage, 1980).

7. S. Levitan, *Programs in Aid of the Poor*, 6th ed. (Baltimore, MD: Johns Hopkins University Press, 1990).

8. Joint Center for Housing Studies of Harvard University (JCH), *America's Rental Housing: Evolving Markets and Needs* (Cambridge, MA: Joint Center for Housing Studies of Harvard University, 2013), 7, http://www.jchs.harvard.edu/sites/jchs.harvard.edu/files/jchs_americas_rental_housing_2013_1_0.pdf.

9. JCH, *America's Rental Housing*, 7.

4. THE INCOME TO LIVE AND
AVOID HOMELESSNESS

1. This an extremely relative statement. The highest benefits available to these subjects were in a few cases retirement pensions from Social Security or the Veterans Administration, and second Social Security disability. These ranged from about $1,000 a month to the highest being perhaps $2,000. These are very small sums for these cities, but are well above what other benefits such as general assistance or TANF or SSI would provide.

2. D. Wagner, "Beyond the Pathologizing of Non-Work," *Social Work* 39, no. 6 (1994): 718–27.

3. D. Snow and L. Anderson, *Down on Their Luck: A Study of Homeless Street People* (Berkeley: University of California Press, 1993).

4. H. Gans, "The Positive Functions of Poverty," *American Journal of Sociology* 78, no. 2 (September 1972): 275–89.

5. G. Dordick, *Something Left to Lose* (Philadelphia: Temple University Press, 1997); and A. Marvasti, *Being Homeless: Textual and Narrative Constructions* (Lanham, MD: Lexington, 2003).

6. S. Sered and R. Fernandopulle, *Uninsured in America: Life and Death in the Land of Opportunity* (Berkeley: University of California Press, 2007).

7. I. Floyd and L. Schott, "TANF Cash Benefits Have Fallen by More Than 20 Percent in Most States and Continue to Erode," Washington, DC: Center on Budget and Policy Priorities, October 15, 2015, https://www.chn.org/topic/cbpp-tanf-cash-benefits-fallen-20-percent-states-.

8. S. Levitan, G. Mangum, and S. L. Mangum, *Programs in Aid of the Poor*, 8th ed. (Baltimore, MD: Johns Hopkins University Press, 2003).

9. US Social Security Administration, *Monthly Statistical Snapshot*, https://www.ssa.gov/policy/docs/quickfacts/stat_snapshot.

10. NOLO, *Disability Secrets*, https://www.disabilitysecrets.com.

11. US Social Security Administration, *Monthly Statistical Snapshot*.

12. A. Delaney and A. Schiller, "A Lot Fewer Americans Get Unemployment Benefits Than You Think," *Huffington Post*, March 13, 2015, accessed September 5, 2016, https://www.huffingtonpost.com/2015/03/13/unemployment-benefits-rate_n_6832552.html.

13. M. Ford, *The Rise of Robots: Technology and the Jobless Future* (New York: Basic, 2015).

5. COMMUNITY, SUPPORT, AND
STAYING HOUSED

1. In this study, the friends made in "informal systems" such as the neighborhood, whether on the streets or at the places people previously lived, were less significant (or at least less talked about) than the formal organizations in some of the subjects' lives.

2. P. T. Yanos, B. J. Felton, S. Tsemberis, and V. A. Frye, "Exploring the Role of Housing Type, Neighborhood Characteristics, and Lifestyle Factors in Community Integration of Formerly Homeless Persons Diagnosed with Mental Illness," *Journal of Mental Health* 16, no. 6 (2007): 703–17.

3. Yanos, Felton, Tsemberis, and Frye, "Exploring the Role of Housing Type."

4. R. Fisher, *Let the People Decide: Neighborhood Organizing in America* (Toronto: Twayne, 1994).

5. R. Putnam, *Bowling Alone: The Collapse and Revival of American Community* (New York: Simon & Schuster, 2000).

6. V. Oliver and R. Cheff, "The Social Network: Homeless Young Women, Social Capital, and the Health Implications of Belonging Outside the Nuclear Family," *Youth and Society* 46, no. 5 (2014): 642–62.

7. Putnam, *Bowling Alone*.

8. W. Whyte, *Street Corner Society: The Social Structure of the Italian Slum* (Chicago: University of Chicago Press, 1943); E. Liebow, *Tally's Corner* (Boston: Little, Brown, 1967); C. Stack, *All My Kin: Strategies for Survival in the Black Community* (New York: Harper and Row, 1974); W. Kornblum, *Blue Collar Community* (Chicago: University of Chicago Press, 1974); D. Wagner, *Checkerboard Square: Culture and Resistance in a Homeless Community* (Boulder, CO: Westview, 1993); and P. Bourgeois, *In Search of Respect: Selling Crack in El Barrio* (Cambridge, UK: Cambridge University Press, 1995).

9. Wagner, *Checkerboard Square*.

10. T. Yosso, "Whose Culture Has Capital? A Critical Race Theory Discussion of Community Cultural Wealth," *Race Ethnicity and Education* 8, no. 1 (March 2006): 69–91.

11. Wagner, *Checkerboard Square*.

12. Stack, *All My Kin*.

13. W. J. Wilson, *More Than Just Race: Being Black and Poor in the Inner City* (New York: Norton, 2004); Wilson, *The Truly Disadvantaged: The Inner City, the Underclass, and Public Policy* (Chicago: University of Chicago Press, 1987); Wilson, *When Work Disappears: The World of the New Urban Poor* (New York: Knopf, 1996); and W. J. Wilson and R. Taub, *There Goes the*

Neighborhood: Racial, Ethnic, and Class Tensions in Four Chicago Neighborhoods and Their Meaning for America (New York: Knopf, 2006).

14. D. Wagner and M. Cohen, "The Power of the People: Homeless Protesters in the Aftermath of Social Movement Participation," *Social Problems* 38, no. 4 (1991): 543–61.

15. Wagner and Cohen, "The Power of the People."

16. Wagner and Cohen, "The Power of the People."

17. D. Foss and R. Larkin, *Beyond Revolution: A New Theory of Social Movements* (New York: Praeger, 1986).

18. R. Whitley, M. Harris, R. Fallot, and R. Berley, "The Active Ingredients of Intentional Recovery Communities and the Implications for Urban Schooling," *School Community Journal* 24, no. 2 (2008): 33–62; and I. Kawachi and L. F. Berkman, "Social Ties and Mental Health," *Journal of Urban Health: Bulletin of the New York Academy of Medicine* 78, no. 3 (2001): 458–67.

19. Whitley, Harris, Fallot and Berley, "The Active Ingredients of Intentional Recovery Communities."

20. Putnam, *Bowling Alone.*

21. T. J. Melish, "Maximum Feasible Participation of the Poor: New Governance, New Accountability, and a 21st Century War on the Sources of Poverty," *Yale Human Rights and Development Journal* 13, no. 1 (2014): 1–135.

22. *Tent City, U.S.A.* (New York: Oprah Winfrey Network, 2012).

23. S. Hamada and S. Sinkle, *Inside Life Outside* (New York: New Day Films, 1988).

24. Erving Goffman, *Stigma: Notes on the Management of Spoiled Identity* (Englewood Cliffs, NJ: Prentice-Hall, 1965).

6. THE THERAPEUTIC ROAD TO RECOVERY

1. R. Bellah and R. Madsen, *Habits of the Heart: Individualism and Commitment in American Life* (New York: Harper and Row, 1985).

2. H. Hutchins and S. Kirk, *Making Us Crazy: DSM: The Psychiatric Bible and the Creation of Mental Disorders* (New York: Free Press, 1997).

3. Many books on counseling and race, gender, and class indicate that nonwhites are very infrequent users of therapy and counseling; see L. Davis and E. Proctor, *Race, Class, and Gender: Guidelines for Practice with Individuals, Families, and Groups* (Englewood Cliffs, NJ: Prentice-Hall, 1989); recent articles on African Americans include M. Williams, "Why African Americans Avoid Psychotherapy," *Psychology Today*, November 2, 2011, https://www.psychologytoday.com/blog/culturally-speaking/201111/why-african-americans-

avoid-psychotherapy and M. Parker, "How to Stay Sane While Black," *New York Times* Sunday Review Section, November 19, 2016; for Latinos see M. Carteret, "Addressing Disparities in Mental Health Care for Latinos," *Dimensions of Culture: Cross-Cultural Communications for Healthcare Professionals* (blog), May 2016, http://www.dimensionsofculture.com/2016/05/addressing-disparities-in-mental-health-care-for-latinos.

4. I was surprised how many subjects, particularly in Los Angeles and Washington, DC, mentioned seeing psychiatrists. In my experience in the Northeast, homeless and even formerly homeless people, if they consult a counselor at all, are likely to see a social worker. Psychiatry has tended to handle only medication issues. It is difficult to tell whether state rules and practices are different as to which practitioners see clients, whether the subjects are referring to non-psychiatrists as psychiatrists or therapists, or if they were seen for one-shot "psychiatric consults," which are usually reimbursed in most states if deemed necessary.

5. New Age concepts and trappings have many definitions. Thus recovery usually shares a spiritual emphasis of an alternative kind from mainstream religions and draws from many philosophical and metaphysical influences from the Native American culture through the counterculture. Reggie and Mary are two of five subjects, all in California, who drew heavily on this influence. Although not all of the subjects used *recovery* as a term, the personalistic view of their lives with an emphasis on healing from toxic influences was quite similar to substance use and mental health and recovery discourses.

6. Anyone may attend LACAN meetings, so this is not to indicate necessary agreement.

7. R. Bellah and R. Madsen, *Habits of the Heart: Individualism and Commitment in American Life* (New York: Harper and Row, 1985).

8. Bellah and Madsen, *Habits of the Heart*.

9. LACAN and other groups have waged a campaign against SCI, and the city seems to have quietly terminated it. See also F. Stuart, "How Zero-Tolerance Policing Pits Poor against Poor: Lessons from Los Angeles' Skid Row," *Mother Jones*, August 1, 2016.

10. G. Holland, "Plans for Skid Row Restaurant Concern Some Residents," *Los Angeles Times*, December 25, 2013.

11. G. Holland, "Alcohol Permit Denied for Eatery in Building That Serves Homeless," *Los Angeles Times*, March 13, 2014.

12. Holland, "Alcohol Permit Denied."

13. D. Forbes, *False Fixes: The Cultural Politics of Drugs, Alcohol, and Addictive Relations* (Albany: State University of New York Press, 1994).

14. The discussion of the drug war among progressives has emphasized a disproportionate number of arrests in African American and (sometimes) Lati-

no areas, which is true. However, the tendency to compare these numbers with data on drugs that comes from self-reported use by adolescents or adults does not tell us much. Mostly this data asks if those surveyed have *ever* used drugs. The response rate is relatively high and particularly among white and affluent populations. However, this does not indicate addiction or even problem usage of drugs. In my view, the drug war should be opposed as very bad social policy whatever the disproportionate effects are, and even if these effects were somehow eradicated.

15. J. Malapde, *Agents and Assets*, http://www.lapovertydept.org/agents-and-assets-cleveland; this play was first produced in Cleveland, Ohio in 2004. It is widely commented on in Skid Row as well as other African American communities that the crack epidemic (and perhaps other drug surges) was promoted by government. Some say the same about HIV-AIDS. While these sentiments are understandable, they have become a sort of urban myth not subject to much empirical support.

16. D. Wagner, *Checkerboard Square: Culture and Resistance in a Homeless Community*. Boulder, CO: Westview, 1993.

17. See for example H. Miller, *On the Fringe: The Dispossessed in America* (Lexington, MA: D. C. Heath, 1991); R. H. Roper, *The Invisible Homeless: A New Urban Ecology* (New York: Human Science Press, 1988); R. Rosenthal, *Homeless in Paradise* (Philadelphia: Temple University Press, 1994); and T. Wright, *Out of Place: Homeless Mobilizations, Subcities and Contested Landscapes* (Albany, NY: SUNY Press, 1997).

18. Figures range widely and often add mentally ill and substance-using homeless showing huge rates such as 60 percent or more. The estimates are not necessarily comparable and because my study explored periods before and after homelessness, it becomes even more complex. I do not argue a causal link here, although obviously some subjects did. However, I would guess that the high number of former users and people with psychiatric issues was most influenced by sample issues. In Washington, DC, homeless activists were interviewed in a focus group and greatly identified around mental health issues, and in Portland, Maine, some of the subjects were identified through social agencies. Los Angeles, while including many people with these issues because it was the largest group, also had the largest number who did not identify with mental illness and substance use. The smaller number, from Haverhill, Massachusetts, and Portsmouth, New Hampshire, were also more mixed.

19. Two subjects had an unknown number of time housed either due to conflict in the subject's statement or failure to provide a clear answer.

APPENDIX I

1. W. Whyte, *Street Corner Society: The Social Structure of the Italian Slum* (Chicago: University of Chicago Press, 1943); W. Kornblum, *Blue Collar Community* (Chicago: University of Chicago Press, 1974); E. Liebow, *Tally's Corner* (Boston: Little, Brown, 1967); and C. Stack, *All My Kin: Strategies for Survival in the Black Community* (New York: Harper and Row, 1974).

2. G. Dordick, *Something Left to Lose* (Philadelphia: Temple University Press, 1997); M. E. Hombs and M. Snyder, *Homelessness in America: The Forced March to Nowhere* (Washington, DC: Community for Creative Non-Violence, 1983); M. Hope and J. Young, *The Faces of Homelessness* (Lexington, MA: D. C. Heath, 1986); C. Jencks, *The Homeless* (Cambridge, MA: Harvard University Press, 1994); E. Liebow, *Tell Them Who I Am: The Lives of Homeless Women* (New York: Free Press, 1993); T. Pippert, *Road Dogs and Loners: Family Relationships among Homeless Men* (Lanham, MD: Lexington, 2007); R. Rosenthal, *Homeless in Paradise* (Philadelphia: Temple University Press, 1994); D. Snow and L. Anderson, *Down on Their Luck: A Study of Homeless Street People* (Berkeley: University of California Press, 1993); D. Timmer, S. Eitzen, and K. Talley, *Paths to Homelessness* (Boulder, CO: Westview, 1994); D. Wagner, *Checkerboard Square: Culture and Resistance in a Homeless Community* (Boulder, CO: Westview, 1993); M. Wakin, *Otherwise Homeless: Vehicle Living and the Culture of Homelessness* (Boulder, CO: First Forum, 2013); J. Wasserman and J. Clair, *At Home on the Street: People, Poverty and the Hidden Culture of Homelessness* (Boulder, CO: Lynne Rienner, 2009); and T. Wright, *Out of Place: Homeless Mobilizations, Subcities and Contested Landscapes* (Albany, NY: SUNY Press, 1997).

3. In Portsmouth, NH, the organization named asked some people who had previously been their clients if they wished to speak with me, and in the Haverhill, MA, area, similarly the agency developed from workers a list of recent or previous clients who would speak with me.

4. US Department of Housing and Urban Development (HUD), *The 2015 Annual Assessment Report on the Homeless*, https://www.hudexchange.info/resources/documents/2015-AHAR-Part-1.pdf.

5. I have followed the convention of how both government and homeless advocates label race and ethnicity. Race is self-identified and does not always follow looks, and ethnicity is really not asked about except in the case of Hispanic and Latino or Asian-Pacific Islander. A sociological view of ethnicity would include, of course, white ethnicity and also black ethnicity.

6. It is my impression from speaking with workers in Skid Row that the area is often more seen as an African American area, although there are Hispanic and white residents. Many Hispanic/Latino homeless people are spread

around this majority Latino city on the streets, in tents and other enclosures, and in predominantly Spanish neighborhoods.

APPENDIX II

1. D. Wagner, *Unlikely Fame: Poor People Who Made History* (Boulder, CO: Paradigm, 2014).

2. A. Kershaw, *Jack London: A Life* (New York: St. Martin's Griffin, 1997), xiii.

3. Kershaw, *Jack London*, 17.

4. Kershaw, *Jack London*, 32.

5. J. L. Haley, *Wolf: The Lives of Jack London* (New York: Basic, 2010).

6. C. Chaplin, *My Autobiography* (New York: Simon and Schuster, 1964), 7.

7. Chaplin, *My Autobiography*, 26.

8. Chaplin, *My Autobiography*, 29.

9. Chaplin, *My Autobiography*, 206.

10. Chaplin, *My Autobiography*, 50.

11. Chaplin quoted in D. Robinson, *Chaplin: His Life and Art* (New York: Da Capo, 1994), 203.

12. Robinson, *Chaplin*, 213.

13. Chaplin, *My Autobiography*, 146.

14. S. Ross, *Hollywood Left and Right* (Oxford, UK: Oxford University Press, 2011), 12.

15. Robinson, *Chaplin*, 124.

16. Robinson, *Chaplin*, 152.

17. D. Wagner, *Confronting Homelessness: Poverty, Politics, and the Failure of Social Policy* (Boulder, CO: Lynne Rienner, 2012); Wagner, *Unlikely Fame*.

18. *American National Biography Online (ANB)* (Oxford, UK: Oxford University Press, 2010), www.anb.org.

19. *ANB* 2010; Wagner, *Unlikely Fame*.

20. *ANB* 2010; Wagner, *Unlikely Fame*.

21. *ANB* 2010; Wagner, *Unlikely Fame*.

22. *ANB* 2010.

23. J. Smith and N. Walter, "17 Rich and Famous People Who Were Once Homeless," accessed December 5, 2015, http://www.businessinsider.com/rich-and-famous-people-who-were-homeless-2015-10; KCRA News, http://www.kcra.com.

BIBLIOGRAPHY

Alexander, M. *The New Jim Crow: Mass Incarceration in the Age of Colorblindness*. New York: New Press, 2012.

American National Biography Online (ANB). Oxford, UK: Oxford University Press, 2010, http://www.anb.org.

Bawden, C. "Homelessness and Domestic Violence." *Parity* 22, no. 10 (2009): 1032–47.

Bellah, R., and R. Madsen. *Habits of the Heart: Individualism and Commitment in American Life*. New York: Harper and Row, 1985.

Benavie, A. *Drugs: America's Holy War*. New York: Routledge, 2009.

Bennett, L., J. Smith, and P. Wright. *Where are Poor People to Live? Transforming Public Housing Communities*. New York: M.E. Sharp, 2006.

Blau, J. *The Visible Poor: Homelessness in the United States*. New York: Oxford University Press, 1992.

Bloom, N. D., and F. Umbach. *Public Housing Myths: Perception, Reality, and Social Policy*. Ithaca, NY: Cornell University Press, 2015.

Bluestone, B., and B. Harrison. *The Deindustrialization of America*. New York: Basic, 1982.

Bogard, C. *Seasons Such as These: How Homelessness Took Shape in America*. New York: Aldine De Gruyter, 2003.

Bonugli, R., J. Lesser, and S. Escandon. "'The Second Thing to Hell Is Living Under That Bridge:' Narratives of Women Living with Victimization, Serious Mental Illness, and in Homelessness." *Issues in Mental Health Nursing* 34, no. 11 (2013): 827–35.

Bourgeois, P. *In Search of Respect: Selling Crack in El Barrio*. Cambridge, UK: Cambridge University Press, 1995.

Broder, S. *Tramps, Unfit Mothers, and Neglected Children: Negotiating the Family in Nineteenth Century*. Philadelphia: University of Pennsylvania Press, 2002.

Burt, M. *Over the Edge: The Growth of Homelessness in the 1980s*. New York: Russell Sage Foundation, 1993.

Byrne, M. "Hundreds of Mainers Line Up for Housing Assistance." *Portland Press Herald*, April 10, 2013, 1.

Carteret, M. "Addressing Disparities in Mental Health Care for Latinos." *Dimensions of Culture: Cross-Cultural Communications for Healthcare Professionals* (blog), May 2016. http://www.dimensionsofculture.com/2016/05/addressing-disparities-in-mental-health-care-for-latinos.

Chaplin, C. *My Autobiography*. New York: Simon and Schuster, 1964.

Conlin, J. "For the Formerly Homeless: Homey Touches." *New York Times*, June 14, 2012, 2.

Cress, D., and D. Snow. "Mobilization at the Margins: Resources, Benefactors, and the Viability of Homeless Social Movement Organizations." *American Sociological Review* 61, no. 6 (December 1996): 1089–1109.

———. "The Outcomes of Homeless Mobilization: The Influence of Organization, Disruption, Political Mediation, and Framing." *American Journal of Sociology* 105, no. 4 (January 2000): 1063–1104.

Cresswell, T. *The Tramp in America*. London: Reaktion, 2001.

Davis, L., and E. Proctor. *Race, Class, and Gender: Guidelines for Practice with Individuals, Families, and Groups*. Englewood Cliffs, NJ: Prentice-Hall, 1989.

Delaney, A., and A. Schiller. "A Lot Fewer Americans Get Unemployment Benefits Than You Think." *Huffington Post*, March 13, 2015. Accessed September 5, 2016. https://www.huffingtonpost.com/2015/03/13/unemployment-benefits-rate_n_6832552.html.

Desmond, M. *Evicted: Poverty and Profit in the American City*. New York: Broadway, 2016.

Deutsch, A. *The Mentally Ill in America: Their Care and Treatment from Colonial Times*. New York: Columbia University Press, 1949.

Dordick, G. *Something Left to Lose*. Philadelphia: Temple University Press, 1997.

Erikson, E. H. *Identity and the Life Cycle* . New York: Norton, 1980.

Eligon, J. "An Indelible Black-and-White Line." *New York Times*, August 8, 2015.

Farrell, D. C. "Relational Theoretical Foundations and Clinical Practice Methods with People Experiencing Homelessness." In *Relational Social Work Practice with Diverse Populations*, edited by J. B. Rosenberger, 261–82. New York: Springer, 2014.

Fisher, R. *Let the People Decide: Neighborhood Organizing in America*. Toronto: Twayne, 1994.

Floyd, I., and L. Schott. "TANF Cash Benefits Have Fallen by More Than 20 Percent in Most States and Continue to Erode." Washington, DC: Center on Budget and Policy Priorities, October 15, 2015. Accessed May 15, 2016. https://www.chn.org/topic/cbpp-tanf-cash-benefits-fallen-20-percent-states-.

Forbes, D. *False Fixes: T he Cultural Politics of Drugs, Alcohol, and Addictive Relations*. Albany: State University of New York Press, 1994.

Ford, M. *The Rise of Robots: Technology and the Jobless Future*. New York: Basic, 2015.

Foss, D., and R. Larkin. *Beyond Revolution: A New Theory of Social Movements*. New York: Praeger, 1986.

Frazer, E., and K. Hutchings. "Feminism and the Critique of Violence: Negotiating Feminist Political Agency." *Journal of Political Ideologies* 19, no. 2 (2014): 143–63.

Gans, H. "The Positive Functions of Poverty." *American Journal of Sociology* 78, no. 2 (September 1972): 275–89.

Geremek, B. *Poverty: A History*. Oxford, UK: Blackwell, 1994.

Gewirtz, A., D. S. DeGarmo, S. Lee, N. Morrell, and G. August. "Two-Year Outcomes of Early Risers Prevention Trial with Formerly Homeless Families Residing in Supportive Housing." *Journal of Family Psychology* 29, no. 2 (April 2015): 242–52.

Goetz, E. J. *New Deal Ruins: Race, Economic Justice, and Public Housing Policy*. Ithaca, NY: Cornell University Press, 2013.

Goffman, Erving. *Stigma: Notes on the Management of Spoiled Identity*. Englewood Cliffs, NJ: Prentice-Hall, 1965.

Golden, S. *The Women Outside: Meanings and Myths of Homelessness*. Berkeley: University of California Press, 1992.

Haley, J. L. *Wolf: The Lives of Jack London*. New York: Basic, 2010.

Hawkins, R., and C. Abrams. "Disappearing Acts: The Social Networks of Formerly Homeless Individuals with Co-Occurring Disorders." *Social Science and Medicine* 65, no. 10 (2007): 2031–42.

Hays, S. *Flat Broke with Children: Women in the Age of Welfare Reform*. Oxford, UK: Oxford University Press, 2003.

Hill, Glynn A. "Report: Housing Vouchers Are Best Way to Fight Homelessness." *Portland Press Herald*, July 8, 2015, A3.

Hoch, C., and R. Slayton. *New Homeless and Old*. Philadelphia: Temple University Press, 1989.

Holland, G. "Alcohol Permit Denied for Eatery in Building That Serves Homeless." *Los Angeles Times*, March 13, 2014.
———. "Plans for Skid Row Restaurant Concern Some Residents." *Los Angeles Times*, December 25, 2013.
Hombs, M. E., and M. Snyder. *Homelessness in America: The Forced March to Nowhere*. Washington, DC: Community for Creative Non-Violence, 1983.
Hope, M., and J. Young. *The Faces of Homelessness*. Lexington, MA: D. C. Heath, 1986.
Hopper, K. *Reckoning with Homelessness*. Ithaca, NY: Cornell University Press, 2001.
Horwitz, A. *Creating Mental Illness*. Chicago: University of Chicago Press, 2002.
Hutchins, H., and S. Kirk. *Making Us Crazy: DSM: The Psychiatric Bible and the Creation of Mental Disorders*. New York: Free Press, 1997.
Jansson, B. *The Reluctant Welfare State: A History of American Social Welfare Policies*. 7th ed. Pacific Grove, CA: Brooks/Cole, 2004.
Jencks, C. *The Homeless*. Cambridge, MA: Harvard University Press, 1994.
Joint Center for Housing Studies of Harvard University. *America's Rental Housing: Evolving Markets and Needs*. Cambridge, MA: Joint Center for Housing Studies of Harvard University, 2013.
Kawachi, I., and L. F. Berkman. "Social Ties and Mental Health." *Journal of Urban Health: Bulletin of the New York Academy of Medicine* 78, no. 3 (2001): 458–67.
KCRA News. "25 Celebrities Who Were Once Homeless." www.kcra.com.
Kershaw, A. *Jack London: A Life*. New York: St. Martin's Griffin, 1997.
Kidd, S., J. Karabanow, J. Hughes, and F. Tyler. "Brief Report: Youth Pathways out of Homelessness—Preliminary Findings." *Journal of Adolescence* 36, no. 6 (December 2013): 1035–37.
Kornblum, W. *Blue Collar Community*. Chicago: University of Chicago Press, 1974.
Kusmer, K. *Down and Out, On the Road: The Homeless in American History*. Oxford, UK: Oxford University Press, 2002.
Levitan, S. *Programs in Aid of the Poor*. 6th ed. Baltimore, MD: Johns Hopkins University Press, 1990.
Levitan, S., G. Mangum, and S. L. Mangum. *Programs in Aid of the Poor*. 8th ed. Baltimore, MD: Johns Hopkins University Press, 2003.
Liebow, E. *Tally's Corner*. Boston: Little, Brown, 1967.
———. *Tell Them Who I Am: The Lives of Homeless Women*. New York: Free Press, 1993.
Link, B., S. Schwartz, R. Moore, and J. Phelan. "Public Knowledge, Attitudes, and Beliefs about Homeless People: Evidence for Compassion Fatigue?" *American Journal of Community Psychology* 23, no. 4 (1995): 533–55.
Link, B., E. Susser, A. Streve, J. Phelan, R. Moore, and E. Struening. "Lifetime Prevalence of Homelessness in the United States." *American Journal of Public Health* 84, no. 12 (December 1994): 1907–12.
Link, B., and P. Toro. "Images of the Homeless: Public Views and Media Messages." *Housing Policy Debate* 2, no. 3 (1991): 649–82.
Lipsky, M. *Street Level Bureaucracy*. New York: Russell Sage, 1980.
Malosi, E., and G. Hague. "Women, Housing, Homelessness, and Domestic Violence." *Women's Studies International Forum* 20, no. 3 (May–June 1997): 397–409.
Marcuse, P. "Neutralizing Homelessness." *Socialist Review* 18, no. 1 (1988): 69–96.
Marin, P. "Why Are the Homeless Mainly Single Men?" *The Nation*, July 8, 1991, 45–51.
Marvasti, A. *Being Homeless: Textual and Narrative Constructions*. Lanham, MD: Lexington, 2003.
Melish, T. J. "Maximum Feasible Participation of the Poor: New Governance, New Accountability, and a 21st Century War on the Sources of Poverty." *Yale Human Rights and Development Journal* 13, no. 1 (2014): 1–135.
Miller, H. *On the Fringe: The Dispossessed in America*. Lexington, MA: D. C. Heath, 1991.
Mink, G. *Welfare's End*. Ithaca, NY: Cornell University Press, 1998.
National Coalition for the Homeless. *Safety Network*. 1983–2014.
National Economic and Social Rights Initiative, *More Than a Roof*, video, 2010.
New York Times. "Ending Chronic Homelessness." Editorial, March 13, 2002, A24.

NOLO. *Disability Secrets*. https://www.disabilitysecrets.com.

Oliver, V., and R. Cheff. "The Social Network: Homeless Young Women, Social Capital, and the Health Implications of Belonging Outside the Nuclear Family." *Youth and Society* 46, no. 5 (2014): 642–62.

Padgett, D. K., B. T. Smith, B. F. Henwood, and E. Tiderington. "Life Course Adversity in the Lives of Formerly Homeless Persons with Serious Mental Illness: Context and Meaning." *American Journal of Orthopsychiatry* 82, no. 3 (July 2012): 421–30.

Parker, M. "How to Stay Sane While Black." *New York Times* Sunday Review Section, November 19, 2016.

Patterson, A., and R. Tweed. "Escaping Homelessness: Anticipated and Perceived Facilitators." *Journal of Community Psychology* 37, no. 7 (2009): 846–58.

Patterson, M., A. Moniruzzaman, and J. Somers. "Community Participation and Belonging among Formerly Homeless Adults with Mental Illness after 12 Months of Housing First in Vancouver, British Columbia: A Randomized Controlled Trial." *Community Mental Health Journal* 50, no. 5 (2014): 604–11.

Pearce, D. "The Feminization of Poverty: Women, Welfare, and Work." *Urban and Social Change Review* 11, nos. 1–2 (1978): 28–36.

Pew Research Center. "For Most Workers, Real Wages Have Barely Budged for Decades." October 9, 2014.

Phelan, J., and B. Link. "Who Are "the Homeless"? Reconsidering the Stability and Composition of the Homeless Population." *American Journal of Public Health* 89, no. 9 (September 1999): 1334–38.

Pippert, T. *Road Dogs and Loners: Family Relationships among Homeless Men*. Lanham, MD: Lexington, 2007.

Putnam, R. "Bowling Alone: America's Declining Social Capital." *Journal of Democracy* 6, no. 1 (1995): 65–78.

———. *Bowling Alone: The Collapse and Revival of American Community*. New York: Simon & Schuster, 2000.

Raphael-Greenfield, E., and S. Gutman. "Understanding the Lived Experienced of Formerly Homeless Adults as They Transition to Supportive Housing." *Occupational Therapy in Mental Health* 31, no. 1 (January–March 2015): 35–49.

Rainerman, C., and H. Levine, eds. *Crack in America: Demon Drugs and Social Justice*. Berkeley: University of California Press, 1997.

Roberts, S. "Reagan on Homelessness: Many Choose to Live in the Streets." *New York Times*, December 23, 1988, 1.

Robinson, D. *Chaplin: His Life and Art*. New York: Da Capo, 1994.

Roper, R. H. *The Invisible Homeless: A New Urban Ecology*. New York: Human Science Press, 1988.

Rosario, M., E. W. Scrimshaw, and J. Hunter. "Risk Factors for Homelessness among Lesbian, Gay, and Bisexual Youths: A Developmental Milestone Approach." *Children and Youth Services Review* 34, no. 1 (2012): 186–93.

Rosenthal, R. *Homeless in Paradise*. Philadelphia: Temple University Press, 1994.

Ross, S. *Hollywood Left and Right*. Oxford, UK: Oxford University Press, 2011.

Rossi, P. *Down and Out in America: The Origins of Homelessness*. Chicago: University of Chicago Press, 1989.

———. *Without Shelter: Homelessness in the 1980s*. New York: Priority, 1989.

Schneider, D. *The History of Public Welfare in New York State*. Montclair, NJ: Patterson Smith, 1969.

Semuels, A. "The Best Way to End Homelessness." *The Atlantic*, July 11, 2015. Accessed August 15, 2016. https://www.theatlantic.com/business/archive/2015/07/the-best-way-to-end-homelessness/398282.

Sered, S., and R. Fernandopulle. *Uninsured in America: Life and Death in the Land of Opportunity*. Berkeley: University of California Press, 2007.

Shields, T. "Network News Construction of Homelessness: 1980–1993." *Communication Review* 4, no. 2 (2001): 193–218.

Shinn, M., B. Weitzman, D. Stojanovic, J. Knickman, L. Jiminez, L. Duchon, S. James, and D. Krantz. "Predictors of Homelessness among Families in New York City: From Shelter Request to Housing Stability." *American Journal of Public Health* 88, no. 11 (November 1998): 1651–57.

Smith, J., and N. Walter. "17 Rich and Famous People Who Were Once Homeless." Accessed December 5, 2015. http://www.businessinsider.com/rich-and-famous-people-who-were-homeless-2015-10 .

Snow, D., and L. Anderson. *Down on Their Luck: A Study of Homeless Street People*. Berkeley: University of California Press, 1993.

Stack, C. *All My Kin: Strategies for Survival in the Black Community*. New York: Harper and Row, 1974.

Stuart, F. "How Zero-Tolerance Policing Pits Poor against Poor: Lessons from Los Angeles' Skid Row.'" *Mother Jones*, August 1, 2016.

Susser, E., E. L. Struening, and S. Conover. "Childhood Experiences of Homeless Men." *American Journal of Psychiatry* 144, no. 12 (1987): 1599–1601.

Timmer, D., S. Eitzen, and K. Talley. *Paths to Homelessness*. Boulder, CO: Westview, 1994.

Toro, P.A., and D. M. McDonnell. "Beliefs, Attitudes, and Knowledge about Homelessness: A Survey of the General Public." *American Journal of Community Psychology* 20, no. 1 (1992): 53–80.

Toro, P. A., C. Tompsett, S. Lombardo, P. Philippot, H. Nachtergael, B. Galand, N. Schlienz, N. Stammel, Y. Yabar, M. Blume, L. MacKay, and K. Harvey. "Homelessness in Europe and the United States: A Comparison of Prevalence and Public Opinion." *Journal of Social Issues* 63, no. 3 (2007): 505–24.

Trattner, W. *From Poor Law to Welfare State*. London: Free Press, 1984.

Tsai, J., A. Klee, J. Remmele, and L. Harkness. "Life after Supported Housing: A Case Series of Formerly Homeless Clients in the Department of Veterans Affairs-Supportive Housing Program 20 Years Later." *Journal of Community Psychology* 41, no. 8 (November 2013): 1039–46.

US Department of Housing and Urban Development (HUD). *The 2014 Annual Assessment Report on the Homeless*. https://www.hudexchange.info/resources/documents/2014-AHAR-Part1.pdf .

———. *The 2015 Annual Assessment Report on the Homeless*. https://www.hudexchange.info/resources/documents/2015-AHAR-Part-1.pdf .

US Social Security Administration. *Monthly Statistical Snapshot*. https://www.ssa.gov/policy/docs/quickfacts/stat_snapshot .

Van Dourn, L. "Perception of Time and Space of Formerly Homeless People." *Journal of Human Behavior and the Social Environment* 20, no. 2 (2010): 218–38.

Van Leeuwen, J. M., S. Boyle, S. Salomonsen-Sautel, D. N. Baker, J. T. Garcia, A. Hoffman, and C. J. Hopfer. "Lesbian, Gay, and Bisexual Homeless Youth: An Eight-City Public Health Perspective." *Child Welfare* 85, no. 2 (2006): 151–70.

Wagner, D. "Beyond the Pathologizing of Non-Work." *Social Work* 39, no. 6 (1994): 718–27.

———. *Checkerboard Square: Culture and Resistance in a Homeless Community*. Boulder, CO: Westview, 1993.

———. *Confronting Homelessness: Poverty, Politics, and the Failure of Social Policy*. Boulder, CO: Lynne Rienner, 2012.

———. *The Miracle Worker and the Transcendentalist: Ann Sullivan, Franklin Sanborn and the Education of Helen Keller*. Boulder, CO: Paradigm, 2012.

———. *The New Temperance: The American Obsession with Sin and Vice*. Boulder, CO: Westview-Harper Collins, 1997.

———. *Unlikely Fame: Poor People Who Made History*. Boulder, CO: Paradigm, 2014.

Wagner, D., and M. Cohen. "The Power of the People: Homeless Protesters in the Aftermath of Social Movement Participation." *Social Problems* 38, no. 4 (1991): 543–61.

Wagner, D., and P. White. "Breaking the Silence: Homelessness and Race." In *Routledge Handbook on Poverty in the United States*, edited by S. Haymes, M. Vidal de Haymes, and R. Miller. New York: Routledge, 2013.

Wakin, M. *Otherwise Homeless: Vehicle Living and the Culture of Homelessness*. Boulder, CO: First Forum, 2013.

Wasserman, J., and J. Clair. *At Home on the Street: People, Poverty and the Hidden Culture of Homelessness*. Boulder, CO: Lynne Rienner, 2009.

Weissman, B., and G. Leiner. *Home: The Langston Terrace Dwellings*. Washington, DC: Columbia Historical Society, 1991.

Whyte, W. *Street Corner Society: The Social Structure of the Italian Slum*. Chicago: University of Chicago Press, 1943.

Whitley, R., M. Harris, R. Fallot, and R. Berley. "The Active Ingredients of Intentional Recovery Communities and the Implications for Urban Schooling." *School Community Journal* 24, no. 2 (2008): 33–62.

Williams, M. "Why African Americans Avoid Psychotherapy." *Psychology Today* , November 2, 2011. https://www.psychologytoday.com/blog/culturally-speaking/201111/why-african-americans-avoid-psychotherapy .

Wilson, W. J. *More Than Just Race: Being Black and Poor in the Inner City*. New York: Norton, 2004.

———. *The Truly Disadvantaged: The Inner City, the Underclass, and Public Policy*. Chicago: University of Chicago Press, 1987.

———. *When Work Disappears: The World of the New Urban Poor*. New York: Knopf, 1996.

Wilson, W. J., and R. Taub. *There Goes the Neighborhood: Racial, Ethnic, and Class Tensions in Four Chicago Neighborhoods and Their Meaning for America*. New York: Knopf, 2006.

World Health Organization. *Gender Disparities in Mental Health*. Accessed April 27, 2016. http://www.who.int/mental_health/media/en/242.pdf.

Wright, T. *Out of Place: Homeless Mobilizations, Subcities and Contested Landscapes*. Albany, NY: SUNY Press, 1997.

Xia, R. "One in Ten California State Students Are Homeless, Study Says." *Los Angeles Times*, June 20, 2016. Accessed December 24, 2016. http://www.latimes.com/local/lanow/la-me-cal-state-homelessness-20160620-snap-story.html .

Yanos, P. T., B. J. Felton, S. Tsemberis, and V. A. Frye. "Exploring the Role of Housing Type, Neighborhood Characteristics, and Lifestyle Factors in Community Integration of Formerly Homeless Persons Diagnosed with Mental Illness." *Journal of Mental Health* 16, no. 6 (2007): 703–17.

Yosso, T. "Whose Culture Has Capital? A Critical Race Theory Discussion of Community Cultural Wealth." *Race Ethnicity and Education* 8, no. 1 (March 2006): 69–91.

Zonkel, P. "CSU Report: 10% of Students Experience Homelessness." *Long Beach Press Telegram*, February 27, 2016.

INDEX

ABOUT THE AUTHORS

David Wagner is a professor emeritus at the University of Southern Maine. He has worked with homeless people and is the author of nine previous books including *Checkerboard Square: Culture and Resistance in a Homeless Community* and *Confronting Homelessness: Poverty, Politics, and the Failure of Social Policy.* He also has written extensively about poverty in the American past in books such as *The Poorhouse: America's Forgotten Institution* and *Unlikely Fame: Poor People Who Made History.*

Gemma Atticks is a master's student in social work at the University of Southern Maine, and plans to pursue a doctoral degree with a social policy focus.